MORAL
JUDGMENT

MORAL JUDGMENT

Does the Abuse Excuse Threaten Our Legal System?

JAMES Q. WILSON

BasicBooks
A Division of HarperCollins*Publishers*

Published by BasicBooks, A Division of HarperCollins Publishers, Inc.

FIRST EDITION

Designed by Elina D. Nudelman

Library of Congress Cataloging-in-Publication Data
Wilson, James Q.
    Moral judgment : does the abuse excuse threaten our legal system? / by James Q. Wilson.—1st ed.
        p.   cm.
    Includes index.
    ISBN 0-465-03624-4
    1. Criminal liability—United States—Moral and ethical aspects.
2. Criminal liability—Social aspects—United States. 3. Extenuating circumstances—United States. 4. Responsibility. I. Title
KF9235.W55   1997
340'.112—DC21   96-46661

---

97 98 99 00 ❖/RRD 10 9 8 7 6 5 4 3 2 1

CONTENTS

ACKNOWLEDGMENTS

For some years I have on occasion delivered public lectures about crime and criminal justice. I quickly learned that the first three questions that would follow my remarks were, in no particular order, the following: What do you think of gun control? Of drug legalization? Of the death penalty?

In 1995 that all changed. The first—and for many people, the only—question was, How could the Menendez brothers have gotten off? Of course they did not "get off"; the two juries were divided between convicting them for murder and manslaughter, and a retrial was scheduled. But the point remained the same—two rich boys executed their parents for financial gain, and the criminal justice system could not convict them of what they surely deserved, first-degree murder. My audiences were profoundly upset about what they—and I—regarded as an indefensible outcome.

At about the same time journalists and one or two law school professors were making heavy use of such phrases as the "abuse excuse," implying that what happened in one celebrated Los Angeles case was in fact the tip of a very large and mischievous iceberg. As a consequence, when I was invited to deliver the Godkin Lectures at Harvard, I decided to use the occasion to investigate what produced an effect so many people deplored, hoping to discover if it was either idiosyncratic or reflective of some deeper deformation in our laws.

On delivering the lectures at Harvard, I learned again what I have so often forgotten: no matter how the world changes, the intellectual life of Cambridge follows its own stern destiny. The first question after my first lecture was this: What do you think of gun control?

My choice of topic required that a social scientist learn a lot of criminal law and criminal court procedure, an enterprise that proved so taxing that, had I realized in advance how much effort would be required, I probably would have selected a different subject. Lawyers, and especially law school professors, have thought long and hard about the issues that help explain the Menendez outcome. Happily, I had the benefit of good advice from four law school professors who read some drafts and gave me clear and often blunt assessments of my ideas. I wish to acknowledge their great assistance: Peter Arenella of the University of California at Los Angeles, Susan Estrich of the University of Southern California, George Fletcher of Columbia University, and Stephen Morse of the University of Pennsylvania. The final manuscript was carefully read by Kent Scheidegger, legal director of the Criminal Justice Legal Foundation, and by Gary Katzman. I also benefited from discussions of these matters with Judge Diane Wayne, former Los Angeles district attorney Ira Reiner, and assistant district attorney David Conn.

I am grateful to many people who helped introduce me to English criminal law, but especially to Anne Rafferty, Q.C., chairman of the Criminal Bar Association of England and Wales, Professor Martin Wiener of Rice University, and Loretta Damron at the London office of the Pepperdine University Law School.

Daniel Garstka was an intelligent and industrious research assistant who not only supplied me with facts but challenged, where necessary, my own views.

Certain errors in my treatment no doubt persist. I apologize to my advisers but take a certain pride in having willfully retained them.

Finally, time away from teaching was financed by a grant from the Lynde and Harry Bradley Foundation, and research expenses were defrayed by funds from the Alfred Sloan Foundation. I am most grateful to both organizations.

1
Faulty Experts

Many Americans worry that the moral order that once held the nation together has come unraveled. Despite freedom and prosperity—or worse, perhaps because of freedom and prosperity—a crucial part of the moral order, a sense of personal responsibility, has withered under the attack of personal self-indulgence.

By responsible people I mean accountable: We ought to answer for our own actions and not, save for the extaordinary reasons, claim that we were compelled to act badly by forces over which we had little control. We all know that society helps shape our character, but most of us deny that society excuses it. People ought to own up to what they do and accept the consequences of their actions. High rates of crime, the prevalence of drug abuse, and the large number of fathers who desert children and women who bore them all support the popular belief that responsibility has given way to selfishness.

Nowhere does the problem of personal responsibility seem greater than in the criminal law. The public worries that criminals are too often excused rather than punished or, if they are punished, that the sentence is too short when imposed and even shorter in practice. The public suspects that criminal trials, especially those involving murderers, have been hamstrung by the introduction of a range of implausible excuses. These range from the so-called Twinkie Defense, a claim of judgment impaired by the toxic effects of junk food, through claims of psychosexual abuse used by Erik and Lyle Menendez to produce a hung jury in their first trial, to arguments that a woman may castrate or shoot a brutal husband even though he is asleep. Americans have never been entirely comfortable with the insanity defense as raised by John Hinckley after he shot President Ronald Reagan; that discomfort has been heightened by what people view as an indefensible effort to extend insanity, narrowly defined, to include psychological states described by such terms as "temporary insanity" or "diminished capacity" or by various "syndromes"—premenstrual, postpartum, posttraumatic, and the like. The emergence of these concepts suggest to many people that essential notions of personal responsibility have been weakened by the frivolous use of dubious theories of social causation. The stern task of judging the behavior of a defendant, based on a dispassionate review of the objective evidence, has given way to explaining that behavior on the basis of conflicting theories presented by rival expert witnesses speaking psychobabble.

Experts on criminal justice see the matter quite differently. Though the law reviews are filled with learned and subtle discussions of every new defense claim that is considered by an appellate court, and though some journals overflow with proposals from law students for even more fanciful defenses, law professors are usually inclined to dismiss public anxiety over such novel defense stratagems. The insanity defense, they point out, is rarely raised and even more rarely successful. And a person found to be insane may spend more time in an institution than one convicted of murder. The Twinkie Defense, though it made for interesting headlines, probably played no role in the case of Dan White, accused of shooting two San Francisco officials. New defenses are being introduced, but few of them lead to killers being acquitted; at most, theories about the mental state of the defendant may lead to verdicts of manslaughter rather than murder, and even that occurs only infrequently. The first trial of the Menendez brothers was an anomaly, not at all representative of the great majority of homicide prosecutions. To be sure, the battered-woman syndrome has been introduced into many trials of women who killed their husbands, but such killings are unusual; the syndrome rarely leads to any outcome more questionable than a lenient sentence based on a recognition of grave prior brutality; and, in any event, battered women are entitled to have the jury hear what has befallen them at the hands of a sadistic or out-of-control husband. Finally, all these excuses, defenses, and syndromes can have no greater effect than a jury chooses to give them; if jurors find such arguments compelling, there is no more reason to exclude from the trial these claims than there is to exclude physical evidence.

Though the public is not comfortable with the lawyers' response, there is considerable logic and some evidence behind it. Legal experts—law professors and criminologists—argue that the American criminal justice system is the most punitive in the free world: more likely to convict, more likely to imprison, and more likely to execute than that of any other democratic nation. We are frequently told that the United States incarcerates a higher proportion of its population than any other nation.[1]

In response, many citizens argue that if this is so, it is only because America has vastly more crime than other nations. For each crime committed, they suggest, we still are more likely than other nations to excuse the offender and moderate the penalty.

In fact, both academic experts and ordinary citizens are partially correct. The experts are right to say that we have a higher fraction of our population in prison than do most other nations, but the citizens are right to think that the chances of going to prison for having committed a given violent crime were, at least in the early 1980s, about the same in America, Canada, England, and West Germany.[2] The experts are correct to argue that America imprisons more of its burglars than do many other nations, but the citizens are right to think that this difference may help explain why the American burglary rate is significantly lower than it is in Australia, Canada, England, the Netherlands, or Sweden.[3] The experts are correct to suggest that America hands out stiffer sentences for property crimes than does Canada or England, but the citizens are right to think that American sentences for property crimes have gotten shorter than they were in the 1950s and that sentences for homicide are not only about the same here as in other countries but are also relatively short (in the early 1990s around six years for the nation and around four years in California).[4] The experts are correct to suggest that America has increased the use of prison for drug offenders, but the citizens are right to think that, at least in the states that have been studied, these offenders rarely go to prison just for selling drugs—most have much more serious criminal records.[5] The experts have some grounds for saying that America is a punitive nation, but the citizens are right to suspect that when incarceration is based on crime rates and time served, America handles murderers much as other democratic nations do, is somewhat more punitive toward burglars, and seems to enjoy (perhaps as a result) a lower rate of burglaries than other countries. In short, the crime policies of this country are more complex than most persons imagine.

These complexities are not widely understood and, in any event, pale into insignificance in the context of a particular trial that has caught the public's attention. When Dan White was convicted of murdering two San Francisco public officials, when Bernhard Goetz was exonerated after shooting some black youths, when the first trial of Erik and Lyle Menendez led to hung juries, or when O. J. Simpson was speedily acquitted of his murder charge, what generally happens to murderers becomes much less important than what happens to a particularly notorious one. If there is an acquittal or a light sentence, we are treated to media complaints about the existence of mental conditions and social causes that excuse defendants and to arguments about the influence of race on jury decisions. We are aware that celebrated cases attract skilled attorneys and we suppose—with some reason—that expensive or highly motivated legal talent will produce results that are quite different from those in ordinary cases.

The best defense attorneys will raise the most detailed and persistent objections to prosecutorial arguments, urging every objection that has any support in the rules governing how evidence should be collected, testimony taken, and data processed. Beyond this they will try to portray the defendants as the victims of forces beyond their control—spousal abuse, parental mistreatment, psychological depression, questionable diets, and personal confusion.

Since most citizens have a tough view about crime and its control and regularly join with their fellows in denouncing defendant excuses and judicial leniency, one would expect that most jurors would repeat in their private deliberations the views that animate them in the public square. But repeatedly a remarkable transformation occurs: people who denounce crime as citizens understand, if not excuse, particular crimes as jurors. To some extent this reflects those attitudes we want jurors to display. We hope they will put aside passions and preconceptions, judge each case on its merits, and think dispassionately about what happened. But often our hopes lag well behind the reality: a representative group of jurors, most of whom have feelings about crime no different from those of the average citizen, decides a matter in ways that they would have likely denounced had they stayed out of the jury box.

It is one of the purposes of this book to explain that transformation. I want to explain why jurors often behave in ways that lead citizens to criticize American society for its alleged moral decay. Many of us believe that there has been a decline in the willingness of citizens to assume and ascribe personal responsibility for their actions. In this view we are now more likely to deny guilt, to expect rewards without efforts, to blame society for individual failings, and to exploit legal technicalities to avoid moral culpability.

I wish to assess one count in this indictment—namely, the argument that the legal system has become excessively tolerant of excuses. I will begin with an account of how the law shapes self-control and continue in the next chapter with an analysis of how it defines self-defense. I then will turn to a history of Anglo-Saxon law that briefly explains how we have steadily transformed the rules governing self-control and self-defense. I will end with an explanation of the necessary tension in each of us between the desire to judge and the desire to explain human behavior. Unless the law proceeds carefully, it risks placing its finger too heavily on one side of that tension—typically, the explanatory side—so that juries are more likely to explain and less likely to judge the defendant's actions.

Social science seeks to explain behavior, criminal law to judge it. Science seeks causation and tries to clarify motives; the law demands responsibility and tends to discount motives. The central failing of American criminal law is not the adoption of endless "abuse excuses," but blurring the boundaries between imperfect science and commanding law, with the consequent admission into courts of questionable expert testimony.

The general principle of Anglo-Saxon law is that people are responsible for their actions, but to this rule there have been added, by the combined effects of justice and benevolence, a number of exceptions.[6] For murder these include those based on justifications (such as self-defense), excuses (such as accident or insanity), and mitigations (such as causing a reasonable person to lose his or her self-control).[7] These exceptions, originally designed to moderate severe penalties, such as the execution of all murderers, have created an opportunity for medicine and social science to explain criminal behavior by expanding on what mental states may weaken self-control, enlarging on what constitutes self-defense, and exploring what might amount to a provocation. The result has been a tension between judging and explaining a killing, with the result that in some cases—not as many as some critics allege, but more than most people would accept—we get a criminal law that punishes conduct only to the extent that it was an act of deliberate hostility or arose without the aid of any one of a growing list of temporizing conditions.

The law, we must not forget, holds us all to a high standard: We must never intentionally and without justification harm others, and to conform to that standard we must learn, as Oliver Wendell Holmes put it, not only the law but the lessons of common experience.[8]

The most visible symbol of the growing struggle between science and law is the rise in expert testimony. When we think of an expert, we imagine a person who has a commanding knowledge of a subject about which knowledge, and not merely opinion, is possible. There is, of course, scarcely any such thing as incontrovertible scientific evidence. For nearly every proposition, some future event may disprove or reshape it. "The sun always rises in the east" seems a secure scientific statement, but in the event of an unpredictable celestial holocaust, it may not rise at all, or if it does, there might be no earth left to provide a basis for distinguishing east from west.

Scientists do not know incontrovertible facts; they know, instead, methods by which supposed facts may be tested. Usually, we say that for a statement to be a fact it ought to be possible to disprove it. "The sun rises in the east" must be taken seriously as a putative fact because—who knows?—it might rise someday in the west, or not at all. It becomes more like a real fact than a supposed one the more consistently we observe that despite the daily opportunity for refuting it, it has never (yet) been refuted. The more times a statement might be disproved and yet is not, the more likely we are to regard it as a fact.

This means that real knowledge, as opposed to mere opinion, consists of statements that have survived the efforts of many people to disprove them. Such knowledge need not be scientific; it could as well be practical, of the sort acquired by a carpenter, a plumber, or a bank loan officer. What all such groups know, and not just think, are statements that could be falsified but, in general, are not.[9]

Science is, in a sense, a formal way of exposing assertions to the possibility of being disproved. It includes a host of methods and habits, ranging from careful experimentation through statistical inference to the testing of ideas by rival scientists. Some aspects of what we know about people meet these scientific tests reasonably well. We know that blood circulates, the brain produces weak electrical currents, intelligence is largely but not entirely inherited, and the lack of certain vitamins contributes to specific disorders. Other aspects of people are more problematic: for example, we can tell roughly the difference between types of personality, though there is a lot of uncertainty as to how precisely we can measure the differences and what they imply for human conduct. And still other features of people are much more speculative, such as the relationship between attitudes and behavior; our inclination to help others or seek help for ourselves; and how we respond to crowds, alcohol, and ideology.

For several decades the courts have increased dramatically the extent to which they admit testimony by people claiming to be experts—claiming, that is, that they can make statements that are not easily disproved about the sources of human behavior. Much of this new testimony has been the inevitable result of matters entering the courtroom—such as the effect of a drug on a patient or the precision of DNA testing in identifying blood—that once were not matters of scientific clarity at all.

Under the rules governing federal courts, a judge may allow testimony from an "expert"—defined (quite loosely) as anyone "qualified" by "knowledge, skill, experience, training, or education"—if the judge believes that testimony will assist the judge or jury in understanding the evidence.[10] Lay witnesses in a trial can testify only about what they saw or heard. But when experts testify, they may give their *opinion* on a matter.

Presumably the expert opinion reflects real knowledge and not mere opinion. At one time the federal courts followed a rule—known as the *Frye* rule, after the case in which it was announced in 1923—that required an expert to be someone who could show that what he or she was saying had survived the test of "general acceptance in the particular field in which it belongs."[11] Many state courts continue to use some version of the *Frye* test.

"General acceptance" is a useful test, helpful in distinguishing real from self-proclaimed experts. Carefully applied, it will help us distinguish between absurd quacks with loony ideas and careful scholars with important views. The test has governed many state and federal appellate court decisions. But even courts that use this test may use it in a way that lets in questionable expert evidence. The California Supreme Court in 1989 decided that, though bound by the "general acceptance" rule, it would let a psychologist testify in support of the innocence of persons charged with repeated acts of sexual perversion against children. The psychologist, who had been barred from the trial on the basis of the *Frye* test, wanted to say that after having given two written tests to a defendant in her jail cell and talking to her for about two hours, he was confident she had a "normal personality" and "is falsely charged in this matter." Based on his tests, he found her innocent. In reaching this conclusion, he could cite no studies that proved that the written tests could tell the difference between child abusers and normal people.[12] The test—the Minnesota Multiphasic Personality Inventory (MMPI)—is a widely used and scientifically valuable test, but it cannot possibly ascertain the guilt or innocence of a person, and was never designed to do so. It estimates, but cannot fully depict, someone's personality. And even if it estimates it accurately, an individual's behavior is driven by many forces—an emotional crisis, the influence of others, the consumption of drugs, the prospect of easy gains, a belief in secrecy—in addition to personality. But the Court ordered a new trial in which this "data" would be discussed.

Despite the liberties taken even under the *Frye* test, the Supreme Court has frequently looked for an even more generous rule. Since the mid–1970s the Court has relied on its own Federal Rules of Evidence which offer much broader support for alleged experts. By Rule 702, an expert is anyone who is qualified by "knowledge, skill, experience, training, or education" to offer a useful opinion.[13] Read literally, this could qualify almost anyone who claims to have knowledge and can produce some bits of personal history to show that he or she has acquired it by some means.

This rule, along with the laxity with which some states have applied the *Frye* test, has contributed to the explosion of expert testimony and has made it far easier for attorneys to enlist their own advocates whose qualification may be little more than having an advanced degree. There is no lawyer worth his hire who cannot find an expert to testify in a way that will help his client even though the opposing lawyer has his own expert testifying with equal assurance on the other side.

In 1993 the Supreme Court tried to set some boundaries around this proliferation by issuing an opinion that seemed to establish some principles that would define expertise beyond the expert's claimed education or training. These limits were drawn from the standards of scientific discourse. The Court rejected the old *Frye* test, and instead has urged courts to apply the usual standards that scientists use in deciding what statements to believe: Has it withstood falsification? Does the claim have a low rate of error? Was it published in a scientific journal?

These are admirable sentiments, but they are stated in rather general terms. How do you apply these scientific customs to the reality of legal arguments in real courts? The Court was not very clear on this except to urge judges and lawyers to argue about it: "Vigorous cross-examination, presentation of contrary evidence, and careful instruction on the burden of proof" will tell the jury whom to believe and whom to ignore.[14] In short, lawyers, guided by judges, can settle expert arguments.

Perhaps, but there is so far little evidence of this. In civil and criminal law the tide of rival and confusing expert testimony continues to rise. The heated disputes between rival experts over DNA evidence in the Simpson trial is perhaps the best-known example. Less well known but equally important arguments—arguments with which this book will deal—arise when experts claim to know whether a person's mind has been "diminished" or the extent to which it has been confused by intoxication or battered into helplessness.

Nearly a century ago Judge Learned Hand put the problem quite well: "The trouble with expert testimony is that it is setting the jury to decide, where doctors disagree. . . . But how can the jury judge between two statements founded on an experience admittedly foreign in kind to their own? It is just because they are incompetent for such a task that the expert is necessary at all."[15]

Matters are not quite that bleak in all cases. To exaggerate a good bit, one can distinguish between two kinds of scientific evidence: arguments that have been routinely exposed to the possibility of falsification and have survived those challenges and arguments that have not been so exposed or, if exposed, have often been rejected. Take fingerprints and voiceprints. After years of great effort, we can be pretty certain that a fingerprint identifies a unique person, but we cannot say the same thing about a voiceprints. Or consider blood testing and polygraphs ("lie detectors"). With the advent of the best DNA methods, we are pretty sure that we know whether the suspect left a drop of blood, but despite extensive efforts we are not as confident (if confident at all) that a polygraph has proved that the accused lied.

The distinction between science that has robustly survived falsification and that which has not roughly matches (with many exceptions) the difference between hard science (that is, the scientific method applied to inanimate things and parts of the human body) and social science (that is, the scientific method applied to the whole person or to groups of persons). I am an unashamed social scientist, but I would be the first to admit that though social scientists often know things about human behavior that ordinary folks do not, we also are aware that the human being defies accurate measurement in much of its important behavior; that even when measured, many people behave differently from what the theory predicts; and that some theories, when known to people, lead them to change their behavior in ways that confound the theory.

For example, scholars have shown that ordinary people will often do apparently horrible things to innocent persons if ordered to do so by a person dressed up as a university scientist. But we also know that some people will not do these things and that if you tell people in advance how they are expected to behave, they will change their behavior.[16] People are complex, changeable creatures often better described by good poetry than good science.

This crude distinction between the science of inanimate or subhuman things and the science of human behavior roughly corresponds to the legal difference between establishing whether a person broke the law and why he or she broke it. A fingerprint or DNA test or ballistic analysis of a bullet may put the suspect at the crime; social scientists, however, would like to explain why he was at the scene and what was running through his mind at the time.

Social science can rarely do this. The very best such analysts can ordinarily say usually amounts to little more than this: if one thousand people with the characteristics of the suspect were at the scene of the crime, then 57 percent (or 76 percent or whatever percent) would probably (subject to a 95 percent confidence interval) react to those characteristics in a certain way. This is useful social science, but it is useless legal advice. The law wants to know whether *this person* acted rightly or wrongly, and why. Offering statistical odds about what fraction of a large population would act in a certain way is nearly meaningless as an account of *this person's* actions except in the very unusual case when the odds are so high as to approach the confidence we have in a fingerprint.

This is not to say that hard science makes things easier for a jury and soft science makes them harder. Indeed, matters often run quite the other way. Hard science is often quite complex (consider the difficulty of understanding how we measure DNA); soft science often appears quite easy (we all think we know what a personality disorder is). The jury, by believing social science and being puzzled by hard science, often rejects that which they should accept and accepts that which they should reject.[17]

Consider how an expert witness testified on behalf of the police officers who beat Rodney King in Los Angeles. He said that by looking at each individual frame of the tape recording of four officers beating King, one could see evidence in each frame that might have led them to believe that King's movements were hostile or aggressive. The first jury seemed to believe them. But this was certainly not science and barely constituted expertise. As Professor George Fletcher later remarked, "One man's twitch . . . is another man's threat."[18] If a frame-by-frame analysis showed in each case that King *might* have been hostile in any given frame, then there was no reason to stop after delivering 56 blows; why not 156, or 1,156? Why not beat him until he was entirely unconscious? Frame by frame, King's behavior may have been ambiguous; taken as a whole, the police behavior was unjustifiably severe.

In the same way, expert testimony that a woman was abused by her husband might be based on evidence (though as you will see, there is as yet not much) that a certain percentage of beaten wives become psychologically isolated and so utterly dependent on the abuser that they really believe there is no escape short of his death. There may someday be such science, but it doesn't exist now. But even if there is, does it predict how *this woman* felt in *these circumstances?* Unless social science in the future manages to achieve what it has almost never achieved until now, the answer is almost surely no.

This is the central problem for judges as they grapple with expert witnesses summoned to explain behavior in criminal cases. Except by linking that behavior to a general pattern, and sometimes not even then, we do not know how to explain what a given person does in some particular circumstance. Given that fact (to which there may be a handful of exceptions), the Supreme Court's decision that science is admissible and useful if it has survived falsification is not very helpful.

Worse yet, the trial courts often do not even apply the Court's test. Their practice is to let each attorney introduce "experts" qualified by having advanced degrees, being able to list publications, and having served in other cases as experts. You could as easily assemble an "expert" by throwing a rock through the windows of a social science research building and seeing whom it hit. I have been asked on several occasions to testify as an expert on matters that I had in fact studied, but without any real effort by the attorneys to find out if what I knew was anything more than a general opinion buttressed by an academic reputation. With one (I think defensible) exception, I have always declined.

Consider now what happens when social scientists more willing than I to be labeled an expert testify in court. If they are honest, they will report some general tendencies and then say that they cannot be certain whether the suspect fits those general trends. But this is not what the law wants: the law is not interested in general trends or possible applications, it is interested in clear facts bearing on a specific case.[19] Many experts are all too eager, for reasons of money, ideology, or the fun of the game, to do exactly what the law wants: to speak authoritatively about *a* defendant in *a* case. When one expert testified in the first trial of Erik and Lyle Menendez, she suggested that research on snails could explain why the brothers killed their parents. Their brains had been "rewired" the way, she claimed, a snail's could be.[20]

What are juries to make of all this? As we shall see in the chapters to come, sometimes they make a lot out of it. There may be ways to reduce the impact of ridiculous expert testimony: a judge can rule that the expert is not qualified or, if qualified, may state a general theory about the accused but not offer an opinion on his or her conduct. Some judges do this. But the adversarial nature of our trials makes such rulings hazardous, especially in high-profile cases where determined attorneys are willing to appeal every judicial restriction. Such court-directed remedies are useful, and more should be made of them; indeed, in many states and in the federal system, judges are authorized to do exactly this. That they don't often use their own legal powers is a measure of the extent to which the appellate review process has undercut the rules of evidence.

But I will suggest that a broader issue is at stake: namely, should a judge or jury try at all to explain the behavior of the accused beyond meeting those simple tests (for example, deciding whether his or her actions were self-defense) on which the law has always rested? In exploring the tension between judging and explaining an action, I will be drawing on the work of other scholars, most notably Professor

Michael Moore at the University of Pennsylvania. They may or may not agree with my interpretation, but I wish to acknowledge that my argument, however imperfect, is not original.

If I am correct, then the American and British criminal courts, though they ordinarily confront no complex pleas and few new arguments, have, by the force of history and their own decent-mindedness, embraced a general view that, provided a "deserving" case appears, opens the door to a wider and wider exploration of explanatory theories in their legal proceedings. Do not underestimate the sympathies of judges, especially when sympathy conjoins with the prospect of being sustained on appeal.

For example, under the *Frye* rule, many courts will decline to hear expert testimony about pathological gambling disorders or the effects of hypnosis but, applying the same rule, will accept testimony about rape trauma syndrome or the battered woman syndrome.[21] What are we to make of this? The amount of evidence on any of these matters is, at best, sketchy. The truth is that gamblers and hypnotics seem to have less appeal to judges than do raped or battered women. That may be a distinction, but scientifically it is not a difference. Sometimes things get even worse: a federal court in Georgia held that a spermicide had caused birth defects. The appeals court affirmed, stating that the absence of any science supporting this view did not matter if there was "sufficient evidence of causation in a legal sense."[22]

One wonders how something not caused scientifically is caused legally.

Lawyers understand this matter perfectly and respond by creating stables of highly partisan "expert" witnesses prepared to go the mat on behalf of whatever claim animates the client. Legal reformers would like to change this system, but their recommendations for the most part concern procedure: who picks experts, how do they testify, how are they cross-examined. For matters of hard science, these may be good ideas. But for matters of social science, they fall well short of the mark.

The best-known stories about rival experts come from civil cases because there the stakes are so high that both sides have the motive and the means to invest in experts. Fights over the harms from tobacco or new drugs or silicone breast implants have produced batteries of highly paid rival experts. But matters are very different in criminal trials. Either there is not much expert testimony or, when there is, it is largely introduced by the prosecution. The defendant is often poor, and his attorney may be either paid little or a public defender. DNA testing is expensive, but it is at least reasonably reliable. Psychiatric testimony is also expensive, but it is far less reliable. One psychiatrist, Dr. James Grigson, appearing in a hearing that bore on whether the defendant should be executed, testified that there was a "one hundred percent and absolute" chance that the defendant would kill again.[23] The claim is, of course, utterly specious, all the more so since Dr. Grigson never even examined the defendant, but it was sustained on appeal to the United States Supreme Court. Justice White defended Grigson's testimony, saying that psychiatrists are "not always wrong."[24] This comment reflects a touching faith in the ability of cross-examination to test the merits of expert testimony.

Most forensic laboratories work only for the prosecution because most are part of the criminal justice system. Studies suggest that indigent defendants are much less likely to produce expert testimony than are prosecutors.[25]

In 1985 the Supreme Court held that indigent defendants had a right to expert assistance,[26] but the effect of this ruling has been limited. Some courts restrict this ruling to capital cases, others to psychiatric experts testifying about the insanity defense, and still others require the defendant to show in court that the denial of an expert witness would produce an unfair trial.[27] The federal rules of evidence do not generally allow a defendant's lawyer even to depose—that is, take pretrial testimony from—a prosecutor's expert.[28] Even in death penalty cases many courts deny defense requests for money to pay expert witnesses.[29]

All this means that experts tend to become important only in high-profile criminal cases where either the defendant is wealthy or public-interest groups supply free experts. This helps explain, I think, why the public gets upset about rival experts contesting evidence in some trials and why law professors rejoin that it does not happen very often. Both are right, but from neither point of view is it a happy situation. The public suspects, rightly, that some high-profile experts make extravagant explanatory claims where the defendant can afford it, and the professors bemoan, rightly, the unfairness of limiting experts in routine cases to the prosecution.

There are things judges could do to curtail the more manifest abuses created by partisan or unfairly distributed experts; some will be mentioned at the end of this book. There is even more they could do, however, by banning psychiatric and social-science experts altogether. When a member of these professions testifies that the defendant suffers from a "syndrome," be on guard—the syndrome may not exist, or it may exist but not be applicable to the defendant, or it may be applicable but the consequences of being affected by it in some predictable fashion may be unknown or uncertain. With some exceptions syndrome science is suppositional science, which is to say, it is not science at all.[30]

2
Self-Control

THE WHITE TRIAL

In San Francisco on November 27, 1978, Dan White shot and killed Mayor George Moscone and Supervisor Harvey Milk. Arrested, White promptly confessed. His statement clearly pointed to premeditated murder: he had taken a pistol and extra bullets with him to City Hall, climbed through a window to avoid detection, and reloaded his gun between the shootings. Examined by a psychiatrist immediately after the shootings, White showed no signs of psychosis and seemed able to appreciate the wrongfulness of his act. There was no evidence of insanity, provocation, or self-defense. The police thought it was a dead-bang case of premeditated murder. But the jury thought otherwise: White was convicted only of voluntary manslaughter. He was sentenced to seven years and eight months in prison rather than to life.

This case became famous for the wrong reason—the mention during the trial of Twinkies. It came in the course of expert testimony by a defense witness who argued that White suffered from periodic bouts of depression arising from the pressures of White's job, aggravated, in the words of Dr. Martin Blinder, by White's having ingested "junk food."[1] Thus was the so-called Twinkie Defense born. In fact, the psychological effects of junk food were not explored at any length in the trial, nor is there any reason to believe that the jury attached much importance to Twinkies. The verdict they rendered was based on the concept of diminished or partial capacity. This standard, invented by the California Supreme Court, can be thought of as a psychological condition halfway between insanity and rationality. White, it was claimed, suffered from an abnormal mental condition that rendered him incapable of fully forming a malicious or premeditated intent to kill Moscone and Milk. That condition was depression; if it existed, and if it influenced the jury to retreat from a murder conviction, it is of little consequence whether the source was junk food, job stress, childhood experiences, or genetic predisposition.[2]

Whatever shaped the jury's decision, the White trial ushered in an era of increasing public attention to excuses. Professor Alan Dershowitz has compiled a list of some of the newer ones, including drug or alcohol addiction, battered woman syndrome, black rage defense, XYY chromosome defense, mob mentality defense, pornography defense, posttraumatic stress disorder, premenstrual stress syndrome, rape trauma syndrome, steroid defense, and urban survivor syndrome.[3] New ones appear regularly. Richard Delgado and David Bazelon have proposed the "rotten social background" defense.[4] Dershowitz echoes the feelings of many Americans when he complains of our increasing resort to "the abuse excuse" and other "cop-outs, sob stories, and evasions of responsibility."

This list is, I think, greatly exaggerated. Many of these

excuses, defenses, and syndromes have not worked for the defendants who raised them. Colin Ferguson was convicted of murder for shooting several passengers on the Long Island Railroad despite his lawyers' claim that he was a victim of racism venting black rage. No man in this country has persuaded a court that having an extra Y chromosome excused his criminal act, nor has any man been able to beat a rape charge on the grounds that he had been reading pornography. The bodybuilder who said that his use of steroids explained why he killed his girlfriend did not convince the jury. It is impossible to find a court in which a person charged with possessing heroin got off because he argued that he was an addict.

DIMINISHED RESPONSIBILITY

What really settled White's case was the doctrine of diminished (or partial) responsibility defense. Beginning in 1949 and culminating in 1966, the California Supreme Court asserted that even an intentional killer might be guilty only of manslaughter. If murder required the killer to have malice, an intentional killing where the killer lacked malice would be manslaughter.[5] The court asserted that malice existed only when a person was aware of "the obligation to act within the general body of laws regulating society."[6] In practice this meant that the court had created a kind of halfway house between sanity and insanity. Someone suffered from diminished capacity if he or she was "incapable of harboring malice because of a mental disease, defect, or intoxication. . . ."[7]

In 1964 a fifteen-year-old boy named Ronald Wolff wanted to use his home as a place to which he could lure girls for sexual activity. He decided that his mother was a barrier to his scheme, so he got an ax handle, hit her over the head, and while she struggled choked her to death with his hands. He then turned himself in to the police. After he pled not guilty by reason of insanity, the trial court decided that Ronald was sane, convicted him of the crimes, and sentenced him to life imprisonment accompanied by a recommendation that he be confined in a hospital for the insane. On review the California Supreme Court decided that the jury was entitled to find the boy sane—he had planned his crime, concealed his early attempts, admitted the killing was wrong, and behaved calmly and coherently—but it had great trouble sending what appeared to be a deeply disturbed youngster to life confinement. And so the Supreme Court decided that though Ronald Wolff knew the difference between right and wrong, that knowledge was "vague and detached." As a result he was "not a fully normal or mature, mentally well person," and so his conviction was reduced to second-degree murder.[8]

Two years later the California Supreme Court expanded the rule in the case of William Conley. Conley was convicted of murder for having shot and killed a woman with whom he had once been sexually intimate but who was now leaving him to rejoin her husband. He killed her and her husband after having told his friends that was what he was going to do and having bought a rifle with which to do it. But unlike the young Ronald Wolff, he killed his victims not under any disturbed mental state but while drunk. Accordingly, the court held that Conley, despite having committed a deliberate, premeditated crime, had been wrongly convicted of murder because he had been drunk enough to reduce his capacity to understand fully his obligation to obey the law.

Twelve years later Dan White's conviction for manslaughter was based on these rules, now extended so that mere depression, and not either acute mental illness or deep intoxication, was sufficient to prevent a murder conviction. As Peter Arenella later argued, this view opened the courtroom doors to "virtually unlimited psychiatric testimony" designed in large part to authorize "a more subjective inquiry into the actor's psyche."[9] By its rulings the California Supreme Court had set in motion a process that would require juries to listen to expert testimony on the varying degrees of mental health of offenders in order to match the criminal penalty to the psychological cause of the offense. The appellate courts had thereby set in motion a process that rested on a dubious proposition—namely, that the greater the degree to which a crime was caused by something other than free choice, the lesser the penalty that should attach to it.

Mental disturbance, psychic depression, and intoxication seem to have commended themselves to the state courts as causes of crime, but they are a small portion of all the factors that cause crimes by weakening a person's understanding of his or her obligation to obey the law. The California courts' decisions increasingly required juries to consider experts' conflicting views on the causes of a crime in deciding whether a defendant could premeditate a crime and yet lack the "malice" to appreciate its wrongness.[10] In the political reaction to the White case, the legislature passed a law overturning the diminished capacity defense.

But though the doctrine of diminished capacity is gone from California law, it persists in some other states. And the underlying lesson of the doctrine—that a jury can be urged to consider all of the causes of a criminal act—lingers in

California. For example, at one time committing a crime when caught up in a mob frenzy heightened rather than extenuated one's guilt. It was precisely to convey the seriousness of acting illegally as a group that sheriffs once read aloud the Riot Act, a statute that made it a felony for twelve or more people to assemble unlawfully.[11] Recently, however, mob mentality has been introduced in a criminal trial to make a defendant *less* culpable. When Damian Williams, Henry Watson, and others beat Reginald Denny nearly to death during the Los Angeles riots, the defense argued that persons caught up in a mob frenzy could not have formed the specific intent necessary to sustain a conviction for attempted murder or aggravated mayhem.[12] The jury agreed.

No doubt being part of a mob—whether of Ku Klux Klan members eager to lynch a black, of blacks looking for ways to vent their anger at the acquittal of white police officers, or of shoppers searching for bargains in Filene's Basement—does alter the mental state of the participants, but so do many other factors, such as suffering from depression and posttraumatic stress syndrome, taking high doses of anabolic steroids, watching pornographic movies, being the victim of racist behavior, or drinking too much alcohol.

I am suggesting a rival argument. We are all exposed to temptations, we all on occasion lack self-control; some of us face acute temptations or are remarkably deficient in self-control. It is the task of the law to raise, not lower, the ante in these circumstances. The law is unkind to all of us when we are weak and especially unkind to those of us who are often weak. It ought to be so; it is the task of the law not only to remind us of what is wrong—almost all lawbreakers know they acted wrongly—but also to remind us that we must work hard to conform to the law. Let me try to show this by taking the case of intoxication.

INTOXICATION

People who assault, rape, and murder often do so while under the influence of alcohol or drugs.[13] Being drunk does not excuse one from the crime. The California Penal Code is clear on this score: "No act committed by a person while in a state of voluntary intoxication is less criminal by reason of his having been in that condition."[14] This seems only reasonable; were matters otherwise, people would be encouraged to drink even more than they already do before raping or killing someone in hopes of getting off lightly.

But the law rarely leaves a reasonable judge uncontaminated by complications. The complication here arises out of the concept of intent, in particular the distinction between general and specific intent. For example, in many states rape and sodomy are "general intent crimes," meaning that a person is guilty of the crime if he intended to do that which the law prohibits—namely, rape or sodomize.[15] By contrast, a "specific intent" crime is one in which the defendant must be shown not only to intend a crime but also to intend a further result. For example, assault with intent to rape is often called a "specific intent" crime.

J. Lawrence Guillet had accompanied a woman to a tavern where they drank. He then took her to his house, where they drank some more and he made indecent advances, which she repulsed. She got up off the sofa only to be knocked down by Guillet, who continued, in the words of the Michigan Supreme Court, "his attempt to commit rape." She hit him over the head with a telephone receiver so forcefully and frequently that he required hospitalization. Escaping, she called the police. At the end of the trial, the judge told the jury that intoxication was not a defense to crime. They convicted Guillet of assault with intent to rape. The state supreme court reversed the conviction because the judge had failed to tell the jury that intoxication is a defense to a "specific intent" crime—here, assault *with intent* to rape.[16]

The California Penal Code, like that of many states, makes this distinction a matter of black-letter law: evidence of voluntary intoxication is admissible "on the issue of whether or not the defendant actually formed a required specific intent, premeditated, deliberated, or harbored malice aforethought, when a specific intent crime is charged."[17]

It is not obvious how such a distinction can be maintained or, if it can, why intoxication (or other mental states) are relevant to judging specific intent but not to judging a general one. In fact, the distinction is a fiction designed to help a drunk offender evade full responsibility for his actions. Let us return to the case of Lawrence Guillet. What did the Michigan Supreme Court think he was doing when he pawed at his victim, tore at her clothes, and knocked her down? The court in its own opinion said he was attempting "to commit rape." That surely seems a reasonable inference. If the appellate court believed it was an attempted rape, why should it require the jury to consider that it was not? The distinction between a crime and an attempt is this: if I rape you, I obviously intended it (nobody, I think, does that by accident). But if I *try* to rape you, you must prove that I was really trying. Fine. But is not the best guide to what I was really trying to accomplish the actions in which I engaged? Is there any better evidence of my mental state available than my behavior? In some cases my actions may be ambiguous, but it is hard to think of another interpretation to place on those of Guillet. However, let us suppose that some other interpretation is possible; perhaps his pawing and groping and hitting were meant only to convey a desire to hold her hand or give her a kiss. Is our knowledge that he had been drinking relevant to determining that desire? No more, I think, than knowing his testosterone level, the extent to which he was obsessed with sex, or the power of her perfume. If intent cannot reasonably be inferred from behavior, then ascertaining his inner chemistry will not supply the missing inference.

Finally, let us suppose that his blood alcohol level could be shown to be relevant. Why should we assume that if it has any effect, it must be an exculpatory one? Is it not equally plausible to assume that Guillet drunk formed an intent that Guillet sober would not have formed? Being drunk when you commit a crime is often regarded as depriving a person of the intent to commit a crime; where that rule holds, you cannot be guilty of a crime if a necessary element of that crime is committing it intentionally, willfully, or knowingly.[18] And so a drunk who steals at gunpoint is not guilty of robbery if he was too drunk "to entertain the necessary intent to steal"; one who assaults a woman is not guilty of attempted rape if he was so drunk that he is "unable to entertain the intent to have sexual intercourse" against her will.[19]

Forgive me if I fail to grasp what is being said here. Is a man trying to have sex with a woman ever so drunk as to be unaware that he is trying to have sex with her? And if he *is* aware of it, how can he be said to lack the intent to have sex? By my count about half the states retain intoxication as a defense to a specific intent crime. But a few have ruled by statute or case law that voluntary intoxication cannot excuse a person from a "specific intent" crime, a fact that prompted the authors of a leading legal hornbook, Wayne LaFave and Austin Scott, to criticize this view as "clearly wrong."[20] My view is different. If voluntary intoxication "caused"—that is, made more likely—the offense because it weakened the defendant's normal inhibitions, it should be the case that getting drunk and then breaking the law reveals a willful lack of self-control sufficient to lead us to judge the person as being irresponsible and fully culpable.[21]

One can become uninhibited for countless reasons. If voluntary intoxication can lessen responsibility, you are offering a defense that can readily be extended to any action taken by a person that has the effect of blurring his judgment and weakening his foresight. If getting roaring drunk before I try to rape a woman excuses, or at least mitigates, that offense, what about working myself up into a comparable frenzy by watching a pornographic movie, joining a mob, or participating in a disorienting religious ceremony? One response is that alcoholism, unlike mob rioting or religious fervor, is a disease, perhaps a heritable one, and so the heavy drinker is not responsible for his heavy drinking. Something close to that was uttered by five justices of the Supreme Court: alcoholism is "caused and maintained by something other than the moral fault of the alcoholic."[22] This view will come as a great surprise to the millions of people who drink without becoming alcoholics and the millions more who were once alcoholics but by virtue of such programs as Alcoholics Anonymous are now sober. One would have thought that the law would have recognized those distinctions by rewarding the controlled or recovering drinkers and penalizing the uncontrolled, self-indulgent ones.[23]

The Montana Supreme Court found a way to claim that the United States Constitution guarantees that criminal defendants have a right to claim that their intoxicated condition was relevant to determining whether they had acted "purposely" or "knowingly" in killing their victims. James Egelhoff was convicted of murdering two traveling companions while drunk. Montana law prohibits the use of voluntary intoxication to reduce criminal responsibility. Egelhoff's lawyers persuaded the Montana Supreme Court that it was a violation of the due process clause of the Constitution for a state to prohibit a defendant from using his intoxication to show that he lacked the mental state—the knowledge or purpose—to commit a "deliberate homicide."[24]

The Supreme Court was, by a narrow margin, unpersuaded. By a five-to-four vote, it decided that the Supreme Court can overturn a state's criminal law only if some provision violates a "fundamental principle of justice." In reviewing the history of intoxication as a mitigating factor, it found no clear evidence that such a factor has been regarded as fundamental. Before the nineteenth century, being drunk was either irrelevant or made the crime worse. And today one-fifth of all American states have never adopted or have recently reversed the acceptance of drunkenness as relevant to determining an accused's intentions.[25] Moreover, as I have argued, drunkenness can take many forms: moroseness, violence, stupefaction, or even a socially conditioned "right" response. Given the scientific uncertainty surrounding intoxication, it hardly seems plausible to argue that this condition, in and of itself, should be used in a criminal trial to disprove intent.[26]

STRESS AND DEPRESSION

The problem raised by intoxication reappears in cases of postpartum depression. This afflicts perhaps one fifth of all new mothers. A few women in this condition kill or seriously injure their babies. To what degree should suffering from the "baby blues" constitute an excuse, justifying a verdict of not guilty by reason of insanity? The answer, I think, is that it can be an excuse when the postpartum depression is severe enough to constitute a psychosis, as evidenced by the woman becoming delusional (for example, by believing that her baby was the devil). Perhaps one or two out of ten thousand new mothers may become psychotic.[27] For such women the insanity defense is available and has been used. Barring a delusional state, postpartum depression—ranging from the rather common "maternity blues" through more serious depressive episodes—is no more deserving of consideration as an excusing condition than any other partial responsibility defense.

Such women are in the same position as people asserting that they suffer from posttraumatic stress disorder (PTSD). This condition, prominently associated with military veterans suffering from what was once called "shell shock" or "battle fatigue," can in fact arise out of any severe traumatic event, such as being the victim of torture or an airplane crash. The symptoms include recurring memories or dreams of the traumatic incident, a sense of estrangement from others, loss of memory, irritability, and hypervigilance.[28] These anxiety disorders should constitute a defense against a criminal charge only when the symptoms are so severe as to put the person in a dissociative or hallucinatory state, and courts have recognized extreme forms of PTSD as entitling the defendant to an insanity defense.[29] In one case a Vietnam combat veteran assaulted police officers with a log (which he held as if it were a rifle) under the delusion that the officers were enemy soldiers.[30] In this and similar instances, a normally law-abiding person suddenly explodes into violent action.

But no line can be drawn that attorneys and legal writers will not try to blur. Kathleen Householder was depressed after the birth of her daughter. Frustrated at the noise the infant was making, she hit her with a rock, put her in a plastic bag, and threw her into the river. She told the police her infant had been kidnapped and went on television to urge her return. In time she confessed to the killing. Astonishingly, the prosecution accepted a plea of voluntary manslaughter, and Householder spent twenty-two months in jail. In a later commentary on the case, a law student acknowledged that she was not delusional but suggested that she might have been acquitted had she argued that in her depressed state she "felt compelled to stop the frustration" caused by the baby's noise and that this feeling "prevented her from conforming to society's requirements."[31]

Some British court cases have allowed evidence of premenstrual syndrome (PMS) as a mitigating factor to such an extent that it has amounted to a defense against criminal charges. Christine English rammed her boyfriend against a utility pole with her automobile, killing him. Charged with murder, she produced evidence of PMS, was allowed to plead guilty to manslaughter, and received twelve months probation and the loss of her driving license.[32]

Sandie Craddock, a woman with more than thirty criminal convictions, many for assault, stabbed a fellow barmaid to death and was charged with murder. At her trial she claimed to have been suffering from PMS, and her diary certainly confirmed that her past crimes coincided with her menstrual cycle. The charge was reduced to manslaughter, and she was released on probation contingent on her being treated with progesterone. Within two years, as the dosage was progressively reduced, she was arrested again for threatening to kill a police officer. She was found guilty, but because the judge thought PMS was a mitigating factor, she was again given probation.[33] Though a British appeals court made clear that PMS could be used only to mitigate a sentence, not to defend against a criminal charge, the mitigation it permitted—probation for a person who killed another—amounts in practice to a defense.[34]

American judges are to be commended for resisting this line of argument. No one has ever shown that PMS produces a delusional or psychotic state such that a woman in its grasp does not know what she is doing or does not know what she is doing is wrong. Christine English knew she had pinned her boyfriend against a pole and, however angry or depressed she may have been, clearly intended to do it. Sandie Craddock did not stab her fellow worker to death under the mistaken belief that the victim was Margaret Thatcher and that God had ordered her to do it. The mental turmoil experienced by English and Craddock was, no doubt, real enough, but no different in kind from the turmoil produced in men by the excessive use of alcohol or anabolic steroids. It is no defense to say that the behavior of the women was caused by physiological processes over which they had no control while that of the men was the result of decisions to consume dangerous substances. There are, in fact, things that woman can do to control the effects of extreme PMS, as evident in the improvement Craddock briefly enjoyed from progesterone therapy, just as there are things men can do to avoid the effects of steroids or alcohol. The law ought to encourage us, rather sternly, to do these things.

INSANITY

A rejoinder to my argument about these cases is to ask how the rejection of causal theory can be reconciled with the existence of the insanity defense. The law in most states is akin to the M'Naghten Rule: to establish that the accused was insane when he committed the crime, it must be shown that he was acting under such a defect of reason or disease of the mind as "not to know the nature and quality of the act" or, if he did know it, "that he did not know he was doing what was wrong."[35]

Whatever the conceptual ambiguity of this rule, in practice the insanity defense ordinarily comes down to this: is the defendant crazy? In such cases *crazy* usually means "suffering from hallucinations or delusions of the sort produced by schizophrenia."[36] Now the obvious difficulty with this view is that there are many mental disturbances less severe than delusions that might affect people's ability either fully to understand what they are doing or to control their ability to do it. One may be so depressed, enraged, or panicky as to do things that one would not ordinarily do. Mental health is not a bipolar state—crazy or sane—but a continuum, a matter of degree.

That criticism is good science but bad law. It is good science because it points out that all behavior is caused; it is bad law because it implies that to the degree a person's behavior is caused, he is not responsible for it. The effort to enact into law the good science quickly revealed why good science does not make good law. Such reformulations of the insanity defense as that proposed by Judge David Bazelon in the *Durham* case, though they enjoyed some vogue, soon were repudiated in most jurisdictions because they were unworkable. In the *Durham* case Bazelon said that a person was not responsible for his or her actions if they were the product of a mental disease or mental defect.[37] Psychiatrists liked the decision; now there was virtually no criminal trial in which their testimony would not be relevant. Lawyers had a different view, and rightly so. Almost any unusual mental state could become a "disease or defect" and almost any action could be a "product" of that "disease" to the extent the there was even the frailest connection between the two. What had been lost sight of was the commonsense view that people are responsible for their actions unless those actions are caused by a pure reflex or a delusional state utterly beyond rational control. As these criticisms sank in, the *Durham* test was rejected by the courts. In 1984 an act of Congress adopted something close to the old M'Naghten Rule.

The *Durham* decision was the effort of one court to do the impossible—make the law mirror science. It has faded from the scene. What really stands as the current alternative to the M'Naghten Rule is the Model Penal Code developed by the American Law Institute about a year after *Durham* had been decided. The code proposed the "substantial capacity" test: A person is not responsible for a crime if as a result of "mental disease or defect" he lacked "substantial capacity" either to appreciate that his actions were criminal or wrongful or, if he did know it to be wrong, to conform his conduct to what the law requires.[38] The Code makes clear that you cannot claim you have a mental disease or defect only because you have committed a lot of crimes. A serial murderer is not necessarily sick because he has murdered two dozen people.

The substantial capacity test has much to be said for it. It appeals to our commonsense notion that even people who are not delusional—who know the difference between right and wrong—should not be found guilty if they suffer from some mental disorder that renders it impossible for them to know that what they are doing is wrong or, if they know it, to stop from doing it. The authors of the Code do not give any examples of what these mental diseases might be. Surely being delusional—thinking, for example, that your wife is the Devil or your brother is a hostile space alien—is one such disease, but the M'Naghten Rule already covers that. The substantial capacity test requires the jury to decide what other diseases or defects impair what we know and how we act. They are legion, their nature is disputed, and their causes uncertain. To sort matters out, the jury will have to weigh the comments of expert witnesses, with all of the problems that contest entails.

Imperfect as it may be, the M'Naghten Rule, in my judgment, is close to being correct. I believe, along with the psychologist Paul Meehl,[39] that it focuses expert testimony on the issue that they can address with some confidence: is the defendant out of his mind?

Seriously reflection on this issue must begin with a clear recognition of the profound difference between causation and responsibility. One can concede—indeed, if one is an especially ambitious social scientist, one will proclaim—that all human behavior is caused. That is to say, if one knew enough about the antecedent conditions of a given act, one could completely explain that act. "Explain that act" means the following: the observer could construct a theory of why this act occurs that specifies all of the circumstances that are sufficient to produce the act and then test that theory by applying it to a large number of cases in which those circumstances existed. If the theory was never falsified—that is, if the predicted action always occurred—then the action would be deemed completely explained. We might even say that the action was completely explained if the theory was almost always verified, so as to allow for measurement error and other chance events.

For example, if I strike your knee in a certain place with a small hammer, your leg will jerk upward. The patellar reflex is an involuntary act based on a heritable disposition. Things get a good deal more complicated when we attempt to explain intentional thought, speech, and social behavior. But there is no reason to think that these actions are any less caused than the patellar reflex. If we knew enough about my genetic endowment and childhood socialization, the opportunities and incentives available to me and the beliefs and principles by which I evaluate them, we could fully explain why I am sitting here writing this chapter.

But suppose we did fully explain my writing this chapter, or Dan White shooting George Moscone and Harvey Milk, or Damian Williams hitting Reginald Denny with a brick. Would we then say that I, White, and Williams were not responsible for our actions? Clearly not. The reason is not simply that we have no tested theory of human action that predicts these behaviors with much precision. Some day, in fact, we may have such a theory. Nor is the reason that we assign responsibility for these actions that the law rests, of necessity, on a convenient fiction, that of free will, and could not operate if it did not embrace that myth. A legal system and the society it sustains could not long endure if they depended, at their root, on mere fiction. In our daily lives each one of us assigns to others blame and credit for many of their actions, and we do not do this because we are lousy social scientists or eager accomplices in myth maintenance. We do this because we really believe that people can morally be held responsible for all but a relatively small number of actions that are truly involuntary or the product of manifest duress.

Why do we cling so stubbornly to the idea of personal responsibility? One explanation, suggested by Michael Moore, is that to do otherwise is to invite an absurdity. If all behavior is caused by factors beyond the actor's control, and if people cannot be blamed for actions that are the products of factors beyond their control, then nobody can be blamed for anything.[40] This result strikes almost everybody as absurd, and so we reject it.

But on what grounds do we reject it? I suggest it is because we do not use the word *cause* in the same mechanistic sense as do a few philosophers. We recognize that some human action, like the patellar reflex or the epileptic seizure, is caused by processes over which a person has no control. But all intentional human behavior is caused by the interaction of genetic endowment, social learning, and available incentives. The last two components—what we have learned and how we evaluate alternatives—supply us with grounds for rendering one or the other of two judgments: "He knew better" or "He ought to have known better."

When we say, "He knew better," we are saying that his evaluation of the alternatives open to him was morally wrong, and so he could have acted other than as he did. When your ten-year-old son hits his five-year-old sister because he thought you weren't watching, you hold him responsible because "he knew better." When the boy hits the girl because he has always hit her even when you were watching, you (or at least an objective observer) would hold him accountable because "he ought to have known better." But when a one-year-old hits his mother, we say, "He doesn't know any better" and, if we are good parents, we try to teach him to "know better" by restraining his blows and saying, "Don't hit."

When we insist on personal accountability, we insist that people beyond a certain age are moral agents.[41] If they break the law and cannot reasonably claim one of a small number of defenses, then they ought to be held accountable. (I leave open for a moment the question of what constitutes an acceptable excuse and how severe a penalty should follow the finding of accountability.) Not only does this view satisfy our moral conviction that people ought to be responsible for their actions, but it also serves two practical functions: first, it sends a message to people who are learning how to behave that they ought to acquire those habits and beliefs that will facilitate their conformity to the essential rules of civilized conduct; second, a strict view of personal accountability sends a message to individuals choosing between alternative courses of action that there are important consequences that are likely to flow from making a bad choice. In short, what you have learned and how you evaluate consequences will inevitably be part of an explanation of your behavior except for a few compelled actions or wholly involuntary reflexes. Since what you learn and how you evaluate it can be altered, learning and evaluation, though causes of your action, are also part and parcel of your responsibility for that action. Oliver Wendell Holmes put the matter baldly: these limitations on free choice fall most heavily on "those who are most likely to err by temperament, ignorance, or folly."[42]

There are certain conditions that will excuse an otherwise criminal act. They are essentially of two kinds: those that make the act involuntary and those that make it the result of delusion. Being under the threat of death or grave bodily injury are examples of the first kind of excuse; having a defect of reason such that a person cannot tell the difference between reality and delusion or between right and wrong is the meaning of the second.[43]

Dan White was certainly distraught and unhappy; he may have been suffering from depression. Damian Williams and Henry Watson were caught up in a mob frenzy. Patty Hearst was persuaded by her captors to help them rob a bank. But most people who are distraught or depressed do not kill; people in mobs may be rowdy but most do not hit people over the head with bricks; some kidnapping victims may be forced by murderous threats to commit illegal acts, but few are simply persuaded to do so. In short, White, Williams, Watson, and Hearst were not delusional, and no one was holding a gun to their heads.

A complete analysis of the behavior of White, Williams, Watson, and Hearst might convince us that we had explained their behavior and thus that their behavior was entirely "caused." But a cause is not an excuse except insofar as the cause deprives the person of reason or forces the person to act. That is why the law has traditionally limited excuses to clear cases of lack of choice (for example, duress) or lack of reason (for example, insanity). As Michael Moore has put it, no cause is an excuse unless it destroys or seriously impedes our capacity for practical reasoning.[44]

A goal of the legal system is to foster self-control by stigmatizing and punishing its absence. Most people possess enough self-control to refrain from any serious form of criminality. But some observers wish to reduce the punishment of people who seem to lack self-control. There are two things wrong with this. The first is that excusing failures of self-control will increase the frequency of such failures. The second is that once we leave the narrow excuses of duress or insanity, we will have, in the main, a vast list of criminal causes that, if adopted, will erase the distinction between law and science.

Among the causes of crime are a low verbal IQ score; low levels of serotonin and monoamine oxidase; elevated levels of testosterone, lead, and manganese; a heritable predisposition to alcoholism (especially when combined with attention deficit disorder); the presence of the XYY chromosome pattern in men; fetal alcohol and fetal drug syndrome; a mesomorphic-endomorphic body type; a lack of religious involvement; extreme poverty, and living in a single-parent family.[45] In fact, many of these factors have a clearer relationship to criminality than do the factors with which the courts have actually wrestled, such as posttraumatic stress disorder and premenstrual syndrome. Why are some causes recognized and others ignored? I suspect that the chief reason is that some defendants seem more appealing than others—or their defects more tempting.

That those are not good enough reasons will become clearer when we turn to the efforts of Erik and Lyle Menendez to avoid a murder conviction.

3
Self-Defense

On August 20, 1989, Erik and Lyle Menendez shot and killed their parents. In January 1994, after a lengthy trial, the two juries reported that they were hopelessly deadlocked. Half of the jurors favored a murder verdict, the other half a manslaughter one. The deadlock occurred after several members of both juries said that the boys had been the victims of parental abuse that partially excused what they had done. Judge Stanley Weisberg declared a mistrial.

Let us remember who they are and what they did. Two days before the shootings, these grown sons of wealthy parents drove to San Diego to buy shotguns, using false identification. That night they slept in their parents' home. The next morning they exchanged the bird shot ammunition they had bought for more deadly buckshot. That afternoon they accompanied their parents on a boat trip on Southern California waters. (They later claimed that they feared their parents would kill them while they were on the boat, but they went along, voluntarily and unarmed.) Returning to shore, the boys went out for the evening. On their return home they banged on the door to awaken their sleeping parents so they could be let in. The next night they killed them, bursting into their room and firing, reloading, and firing again, fifteen times in all. The final shots were made by pressing the guns' muzzles against their parents heads as they lay bleeding on the floor. After picking up the spent shells and attempting to arrange an alibi (they bought tickets to a movie so they could claim they were in the theater at the time of death), Erik and Lyle called the police and said that they had just arrived home to find their parents' bodies. After collecting the life insurance proceeds, Erik and Lyle went on a $700,000 shopping spree. In time they admitted to the killings but then claimed in court that they had been the victims of sexual and emotional abuse. Roughly half the jurors were convinced and so refused to convict them of murder.

In March 1996, after a lengthy retrial, Erik and Lyle were convicted of first-degree murder. As in the first trial, the defense tried to persuade the jury that the boys had been the victims of psychosexual abuse, but this time they confronted a more effective prosecutor, a courtroom from which television had been banned, and a judge who, strengthened by a new California Supreme Court opinion, restricted the evidence they could use and the verdicts available to the jury. The brothers were sentenced to prison for life.

The first trial did much to convince observers that the criminal law has been corrupted by the easy availability, at least to wealthy defendants, of implausible but effective excuses. Many experts have tried to rebut this cynicism by pointing out, correctly, that only in a tiny number of high-profile cases are such defenses mounted with much effect and that in any event, the Menendez boys remained in jail awaiting a new trial that had, as it turned out, different results. This rejoinder, though accurate, fell on deaf ears. The public sensed that the rarity of high-profile cases does not lessen their philosophical and tutelary significance: it is precisely when all eyes are focused on a case that the law itself, and not simply the defendants, is on trial. If such cases are unique, occurring only when skilled lawyers are employed to stage them, then the law is faulty for being so easily distorted by wealth. If, on the other hand, such trials are but an exaggerated representation of the law's ordinary precepts, then the law is faulty for being badly grounded. Either way, the criminal law has much to answer for.

The Menendez trial was not the first time that jurors were unwilling to return a verdict of premeditated murder despite convincing—I would say, overwhelming—evidence that the defendants carefully planned the homicide. In Wyoming in 1982, Richard John Jahnke, age sixteen, shot and killed his father, Richard Chester Jahnke, after a violent argument. During the several hours that elapsed between the argument and the shooting, the son took the following steps: while his parents were at a restaurant celebrating their anniversary, young Richard changed into dark clothing and positioned several weapons—two shotguns, three rifles, a pistol, and a knife—at strategic places around the home. He armed his sister, Deborah, with an M–1 carbine and instructed her in its use. The son then concealed himself in the darkened garage and awaited his parents return. As his father alighted from the car and approached the garage door, the son fired all six rounds in his 12-gauge shotgun. Four struck the father, and he died. Leaving their mother screaming in the driveway, young Richard and Deborah left the house and went their separate ways.

He was arrested by the police, charged with first-degree

murder, and tried as an adult. The state did not seek the death penalty. After a five-day trial the jury found young Richard guilty—not of premeditated murder, but of voluntary manslaughter. The judge sentenced him to five to fifteen years in prison. The boy then appealed, claiming that the trial judge had erred in not allowing psychiatric testimony about the brutality the son had experienced at the hands of his father. The defense claimed that as a result of this abuse, he became emotionally impaired; he suffered from "battered child syndrome." The Wyoming Supreme Court, by a vote of three to two, rejected this appeal, and Jahnke went off to prison.

In Los Angeles Sociz Junatanov, a boy, had been abused by his father for many years. He and his brother hired a drifter to kill him, but the knife attack did not finish the job. As the father lay recuperating in a hospital, the brother's girlfriend, dressed as a nurse, injected him with a syringe of battery acid. Amazingly, the father survived. Then Sociz approached another man to do the killing; unfortunately, he was an undercover police officer. The girlfriend pleaded guilty and got a five-year sentence; the brother was convicted of attempted manslaughter. But in 1986 Sociz was acquitted of all charges. Later the jury made it clear that they were moved by sympathy for the boy, dislike for the father, and the view that Junatanov came from a "different cultural background."[1]

There were several important differences between the first Menendez trail and the Jahnke and Junatanov cases. José and Kitty Menendez, so far as anyone knows, did not beat their sons; the fathers of Richard Jahnke and Sociz Junatanov certainly did. Erik and Lyle were old enough and affluent enough to live apart from their parents, and Lyle was doing so; Sociz, younger and with fewer resources, lived at home. The Menendez jurors heard weeks of testimony from experts, friends, and teachers about the Menendez family; the Jahnke and Junatov jurors heard from a few experts.

THE LAW OF SELF-DEFENSE

But in one crucial respect the cases were identical: the defendants claimed they acted on a recent modification in the law of self-defense. The law in most states allows people to claim self-defense when they are resisting an imminent attempt to kill or inflict great bodily harm on themselves. But it is not enough merely to fear that one is about to be killed or injured; that fear must be one that a reasonable person would have under the same circumstances.[2]

Each of the elements of the traditional doctrine of self-defense—a reasonable belief in an imminent threat that may be resisted by the use of force proportional to the threat—has been challenged since the mid–1970s by the growing public awareness of the problem of battered women. It is no small problem: men have been inflicting more, and more serious, violence on their wives and lovers than anyone had once supposed. Reading through detailed accounts of this abuse is at once disgusting and enraging, making one wonder just how far out of the cave some men have progressed. The victims of this abuse have become, properly, an object of public concern and scholarly analysis. The changed law and the plight of battered women has had a profound effect on criminal defenses.

The most prominent analyst of battered women was Dr. Lenore Walker, a Denver psychologist who described a condition called the battered woman syndrome and offered her services as an expert witness in cases in which a woman killed her abuser.

Her claims about the syndrome came to judicial notice in the mid-1970s. Here is an early example. In 1976 Beverly Ibn-Tamas shot and killed her husband, Yusef, in his medical office in Washington, D.C. She was convicted of second-degree murder and sentenced to spend one to five years in prison. Beverly testified that she had been subjected to repeated beatings and threats during their four-year marriage. Other witnesses, including Yusef's first wife, also testified to his violent behavior. Events on the day of the shooting were disputed, but what is clear is that Beverly shot Yusef twice, once from close range. Obviously, however, the jury did not think the crime was premeditated (hence a second-degree murder conviction), and the judge found her a sympathetic defendant (hence the short prison sentence). Beverly's lawyers appealed, however, claiming that the court had improperly excluded the testimony of Dr. Walker. A divided appeals court held that it was wrong to exclude Walker's testimony and told the trial court to hold an evidentiary hearing on that issue. It did and concluded that Dr. Walker had not established that her methodology was generally accepted by experts in the field. The conviction was upheld.[3] Beverly served one year in prison.

When expert witnesses offer to testify, the judge must rule on the admissibility of their testimony. In doing so, he or she must answer, among others, these questions: Is the testimony based on facts that are "beyond the ken of the average layman"? Does the expert have sufficient skill and knowledge in this field as to make the testimony valuable to the jury? Will the testimony unduly prejudice the jury?[4] The appeals court said that Dr. Walker's testimony might have "enhanced Mrs. Ibn-Tamas' general credibility" and "supported her testimony" that her husband's behavior had "led her to believe she was in imminent danger."[5] The court compared Beverly Ibn-Tamas to Patty Hearst, who had argued three years earlier in her trial for bank robbery that expert testimony would "explain the effects kidnapping, prolonged incarceration, and psychological and physical abuse may have had on the defendant's mental state at the time of the robbery."[6]

Just what is this "mental state" that is so "beyond the ken of the average layman" that expert testimony describing it is required? The District of Columbia appeals court did not really answer that question, and based on what one can learn from Beverly Ibn-Tamas's trial, the answer in her case seems to be—nothing at all.[7]

A few years later, however, the New Jersey Supreme Court undertook to give an answer in reviewing the case of Gladys Kelly, who had been convicted of reckless manslaughter and sentenced to five years in prison for having stabbed her husband to death with a pair of scissors. Gladys claimed that during their seven-year marriage, her husband, Ernest, had abused her. Though some of her claims were disputed, let us assume they were true. On the fatal day they had a fight on the street that began with an argument over money. Ernest pushed Gladys to the ground, but two men from the crowd separated them. Gladys went off to find her daughter and returned with a pair of scissors she had taken from her purse. At this point the facts are unclear. The defense claimed that Ernest rushed at Gladys with his hands raised and that she, fearing for her safety, stabbed him. The prosecution claimed that Gladys started the fight, chased Ernest after threatening to kill him, and then stabbed him. The state supreme court reversed the conviction because expert testimony by Dr. Lois Veronen about battered women's syndrome had been excluded from the trial.

In reaching this decision, the court drew heavily on amicus briefs filed by the American Civil Liberties Union, the New Jersey Coalition for Battered Women, and the American Psychological Association. It discussed the lamentable extent of wife abuse in the United States, complained of the bias against women that exists in law enforcement agencies charged with investigating abuse cases, and reviewed the theory of battered women's syndrome developed by Dr. Walker and others. As interesting as these observations were, they did not address the central issue: whether expert testimony would have aided the jury in reaching its verdict. Since the jury had refused to convict Gladys of murder (instead agreeing on a verdict of reckless manslaughter), it had already accepted a mitigation, no doubt one arising out of her history and circumstances. And since the judge had sentenced her to the minimum term, he also must have understood that there were mitigating factors. The expert testimony, then, had to be designed to aid the jury in deciding that this was *justifiable* homicide—a case of self-defense.

But what could Dr. Veronen contribute to that issue? Not that Gladys's fear of being killed by Ernest was reasonable; all of the facts bearing on that—and they were disputed facts—were already available to the jury. The supreme court conceded that. The value it found in the proffered testimony was that it would help dispel two "myths": the first consists of the "popular misconception" that battered women are "masochistic and actually enjoy their beatings, that they purposely provoke their husbands into violent behavior"; the second is that "women who remain in battering relationships are free to leave their abusers at any time."[8]

As evidence for the first of these myths, the court cited a book by Dr. Walker. But in fact there is no evidence in Dr. Walker's book that the public believes battered women are masochists who enjoy provoking their husbands.[9] Subsequent research has failed to find such evidence.[10]

The second so-called myth raises a serious question that is not easily answered. No doubt many people, hearing of the abuse a woman has endured, ask themselves why she doesn't simply leave. The explanation advanced by Dr. Walker and others is that battered women suffer from "learned helplessness." The phrase was coined by Professor Martin Seligman, a psychologist at the University of Pennsylvania, after studying the behavior of dogs who were confined in harnesses in such a way that they could not escape painful electrical shocks. They soon ceased to struggle, and when presented with a way out, they chose not to take it. When the experiment was over, they had to be dragged from their cages. The dogs had lost their will to control their environment.[11] Professor Seligman later described depression in humans as learned helplessness.[12] Dr. Walker asserts that women who have experienced the battering cycle—an increase in marital tension, then a physical attack, followed by a period of loving contrition—become helpless in much the same way as do shocked dogs. They believe they can neither control their environment nor predict the effects of their own behavior.[13] Poverty, concern for their children, and the indifference of police and social-welfare agencies may reinforce this sense of helplessness.

No doubt some battered women (and some women who have never been battered) display these symptoms. But the evidence supporting the view that most battered women will feel helpless is sketchy. Mary Ann Dutton, a psychologist deeply sympathetic to the plight of battered women, has written that women exposed to violence and abuse "do not respond similarly" because there is no "singular 'battered woman profile.'" Some feel psychologically trapped and try to stick it out, others solicit help from friends or call the police, still others resist and fight back. Some go to shelters, some do not. Many of these coping strategies turn out to be ineffective, but by choosing them, abused women do not reveal themselves to be as passive as shocked dogs in a cage.[14] Some evidence suggests that it is precisely the most severely abused women who are most likely to leave their husbands.[15] We do not yet have good ways of predicting who will leave a relationship and who will remain helplessly trapped within it.[16]

Moreover, killing one's abuser seems quite inconsistent with the theory of learned helplessness. Seligman's helpless dogs did not bite their abusers, but Walker's helpless women killed theirs. Walker's own evidence seems to contradict her conclusions. A helpless woman should feel that her life is governed by external forces rather than by her own choices, but the battered women Walker studied displayed an internal, not external, locus of control.[17] People who believe that they, and not external forces, govern their lives cannot plausibly be called helpless, especially when in some cases—the women who kill their husbands—they act on that belief.

It would be astonishing if women who have been abused

as much as many of those who kill their husbands did not experience some psychological disorders. There is a good deal of evidence that battered women suffer from depression,[18] though whether that disorder preceded or followed the abuse is not entirely clear. But depression is not a mental condition that, if described by an expert witness, will help a jury determine whether a woman is justified in killing her husband. It is not even a condition that generally qualifies as a mitigating factor.

None of these issues prevented appellate courts from accepting the view that there is a phenomenon called battered women's syndrome about which expert testimony will have significant probative value. (I am struck by the fact that in the vast majority of appellate decisions, the opinion of the court referred, for evidence of the scientific validity and probative value of battered women's syndrome, to other court cases and law-review articles commenting on them. Scarcely any canvassed the scientific literature.) That view has prevailed in many states; in at least nine of them, including California, the legislature has passed laws that allow expert testimony about the syndrome.[19] The California law, for example, says that the syndrome is "scientifically valid," and the Ohio statute added that the syndrome is not only valid but is also not "within the general understanding . . . of the general populace."[20]

In 1996 the California Supreme Court affirmed the legislature's view that battered women's syndrome was admissible in a case where a much-abused woman, Evelyn Humphrey, shot and killed her boyfriend, Albert Hampton, in the heat of a struggle with him. The jury found her guilty of voluntary manslaughter, but the supreme court reversed the conviction because the judge had only allowed the jury to consider whether expert testimony about the syndrome supported her claim that she *actually* believed she was in danger but had refused to let it consider whether that belief was *reasonable*.[21]

It was an odd ruling, one that all the justices supported but that most worried about. By almost any measure, the Humphrey case had raised a straightforward argument: she acted in self-defense. Many of the facts seemed to support her claim. Hampton had been abusive to her for most of the year they had lived together. On the day before the killing, Humphrey said he had tried to shoot her and, indeed, the spent bullet was found where she said it would be. The next day, the man was drunk and abusive. Just before he was killed, he reportedly said that he was going to kill her: "This time, bitch, when I shoot you, I won't miss." They confronted each other at a table on which a gun lay. She said he was reaching for it, but she got there first, and killed him. Immediately afterward she confessed to the police: "I just couldn't take him beating on me no more."

Strangely, the district attorney had charged her with murder, but the judge threw that charge out. The jury was given a choice between second-degree murder, manslaughter, and acquittal on grounds of self-defense. The jury chose manslaughter. The appeal implied that even this was too much; she should have been acquitted. Perhaps so. But the expert testimony could not have settled much on that score. Every fact relevant to convicting or acquitting her was already known to the jury. It could have decided that she feared imminent death and let her go. But it did not; apparently, it was not entirely convinced that she really confronted imminent death.

Dr. Lee Bowker, an advocate of battered women's syndrome, was the expert witness. The supreme court opinion held that his views should have been fully considered to "overcome stereotyped impressions about women who remain in abusive relationships" and to show that a reasonable person in Humphrey's shoes would have felt that she faced a reasonable threat of death. Though six justices agreed to set aside her conviction, most were not very happy with the interpretation that others might put on the ruling. And for good reason—repeatedly court rulings have been stretched to cover dissimilar cases. Justice Brown put it nicely: "For years the lower courts, poised precariously upon the slippery slope of personalized defenses, have tried valiantly not to ski down it."

The problem is to avoid letting claims by experts replace individual accountability. There was very little in Humphrey's case that did not fit squarely within old-fashioned self-defense rules and or that was "beyond the ken" of a jury. By the narrowest of margins, Justice Brown and most of her colleagues was willing to order a new trial to see if a "reasonable person" in Humphrey's position would really feel confronted by an imminent threat of death. The jury will probably be puzzled by this view; almost surely, this is exactly what they had already decided.

The mistaken legislative view that juries must consider the causes of crime has sent the judges down the slippery slope of personalized defenses.

THE PROBLEM OF THE SYNDROME

The position that so many judges and legislators have taken is scientifically suspect, philosophically debatable, and legally unnecessary. The science is suspect for the reasons already stated and others as well: we do not know what proportion of battered women develop a syndrome (and how many develop the syndrome without being battered), and the evidence for the existence of a syndrome was, in the case of Dr. Walker, elicited by interviewers who were predisposed to find it.[22] The American Psychiatric Association has declined to include the syndrome in its *Diagnostic and Statistical Manual (DSM-IV)* despite intense lobbying by its supporters. Dr. Walker herself is an advocate who, though she has interviewed hundreds of abused women and provided us with heart-rending accounts of their misery, displays a tendency to find a "syndrome" when the facts do not support it. When she discovered that many of her women did not display feelings of helplessness and did not have low self-esteem, she expressed surprise and went on to dispute or discount the women's own accounts. She explained that in "reality" these women have no control over their lives, whatever they might say to the contrary; in fact, their denial of helplessness reflects their desire to "gain approval" from Dr. Walker.[23] By 1989, five years after she expressed her surprise at the poor fit between her hypothesis and the data, she had overcome whatever reservations the data had occasioned and now wrote confidently that the "typical battered woman has poor self-image and self-esteem."[24]

Philosophically, it is hard to see why a jury should consider such a syndrome to be an excusing condition if some women (and for all we know, most women) who are battered and who kill their abusers do not suffer from the syndrome. Syndrome sufferers would have the benefit of expert witnesses testifying on their behalf, while equally abused but nonsyndrome women would not.[25] Describing a battered woman as some courts have done—as dependent, brain-washed, terror-stricken, or psychologically paralyzed[26]—reproduces rather than eliminates the very stereotypes to which most of us object. Anne Coughlin states it well: the battered woman claim, designed "ostensibly to refute a variety of misogynist stereotypes," requires accused women "to embrace precisely those insulting stereotypes that the defense was supposed to explode, and it endorses the assumption that women are incapable of the rational self-governance exercised by men."[27] The syndrome defense is, by definition, not available to a woman with a sturdily independent cast of mind and a record of making her own decisions and managing her own affairs. If she kills an abusive mate, she is on her own in claiming self-defense; it is only the passive, weak-willed woman who can use the syndrome to bolster her self-defense claim.[28]

Legally, the syndrome may add something to the traditional claim of self-defense, but that something is ill-defined. It is a mistake to say that the old law of self-defense was inherently masculine. As Professor Susan Estrich has pointed out, the rules of self-defense "exist not so much to define manly behavior as to limit manly instincts—in order to preserve human life."[29] It might be manly, she observes, to respond to a verbal insult with deadly force, but it is illegal because the law requires that there be an imminent danger of death or grave bodily injury. The concern for battered women does, however, raise the following problem: Is it ever justifiable self-defense to kill an oppressor when there is no immediate threat of injury from him—say, when he is sleeping? It is a matter to which I shall return in a moment.

IMPERFECT SELF-DEFENSE

Suppose you honestly fear that you are about to be killed, but that your fear is, in fact, unreasonable. California law, for example, distinguishes between "perfect" and "imperfect" self-defense. In the first case your actions were justified because you killed having an honest *and* reasonable belief of imminent danger; in the second case your actions are partially excused because you had an honest but *un*reasonable belief in the need to defend yourself.[30]

To apply this new rule, a jury must judge only the honesty of the defendant's belief that he was in peril. What is at issue is not the reality of the danger, but rather the sincerity of the defendant's belief in it.

The case that established this view of the California law arose when Charles Flannel shot and killed Charles Daniels in 1976. The two had a history of hostile relations because Flannel was dating Daniels's common-law daughter. In January Flannel attacked Daniels, kicking him in the chest and hitting him with a glass. Instead of prosecuting Flannel, the district attorney warned the two men to avoid each other. Six months later, Daniels arrived outside a building where Flannel was lounging. Though friends urged Flannel to leave, he did not. In the brief confrontation that followed, Daniels backed away. He reached for his pocket where he kept a knife but no gun. Flannel shot Daniels from two feet away and was later arrested.

In deciding the matter, the California Supreme Court held that having an "honest but unreasonable belief that it is necessary to defend oneself from imminent peril to life or great bodily harm negates malice aforethought" so that the charge against Flannel ought to be manslaughter, not murder.[31]

In one sense the rule in the case of Charles Flannel was intuitively satisfying. There is a confrontation between two enemies; they are both emotionally charged; one appears to be reaching into his pocket, where he may carry a gun; the other shoots him dead. Given these facts, some jurors may think that Flannel was guilty of manslaughter, not murder. Against even these facts, however, we must recall that many homicides are the result of such fights between acquaintances.

But the legacy of a rule is often much different from its origins. By the time it was applied to Erik and Lyle Menendez fifteen years later, it had become transformed into the broad concept of imperfect self-defense: any honest fear, however unreasonable, that one's life was in danger seemed to preclude any degree of culpability beyond manslaughter.

Virtually every fact of their case was different from that of Charles Flannel. Flannel had a long history of violent confrontations with Daniels; except on their unsupported claims, Erik and Lyle had none. Flannel and Daniels had a sudden confrontation; Erik and Lyle planned their homicide well in advance. Friends tried to separate Flannel and Daniels; Erik and Lyle acted alone. Flannel saw Daniels reach for his pocket, possibly to get a knife; Erik and Lyle's parents were watching television. Flannel shot once; Erik and Lyle, fifteen times. Flannel awaited the police; Erik and Lyle constructed an elaborate alibi. No matter; however dissimilar the cases, both led to a claim of manslaughter.

It is hard to imagine how a legal philosopher could place these two actions on the same legal plane, and I doubt many have tried. But a jury did—because a judge let the evidence in and because jurors seek explanations to dispel their bewilderment about some defendants' actions that are hard to grasp. When the law seeks to explain behavior, it often blurs the boundary line that separates judgment from explanation.

But suppose that we soften that boundary by admitting a person's subjective condition as a determinative factor in a trial. Take the case of a man who, having been mugged, has decided that the world is an unsafe place, filled with persons—especially young, black males—who will rob and maul at the first opportunity. Accordingly, he carries a concealed pistol. On a subway a young black male approaches him and asks for money. The youth displays no weapon and in fact has neither knife nor gun. The subway car has other people in it. The man does not respond by retreating, summoning aid, or even displaying his pistol; instead, he draws it, shoots the first youth and his companion and then shoots another black youth who had boarded the train with the first one but who had said and done nothing except to attempt flight when the shooting began. After putting a bullet in three of the four youths, the man approaches the fourth and shoots him, saying, "You seem to be all right, here's another." A few days later the man surrenders to the police and states that he is certain that none of the youths had a gun but that he had a fear, based on prior experiences, of being "maimed." He says that he intended to "murder" the youths, "to hurt them, to make them suffer as much as possible."

The man, of course, was Bernhard Goetz. In New York State, where the incident occurred, the law states that the use of deadly force can be justified only when the defendant "reasonably believes" that he is threatened by deadly force or robbery and "reasonably believes" that the use of such force is necessary to avert the threat.

At the end of the trial, the judge defined a "reasonable belief" as one that would be held by a "reasonable person" standing "in [the defendant's] shoes" and facing "the same circumstances and situation" that the he faced. In short, it was not simply Goetz's perceptions that mattered, but rather the perceptions of a reasonable person in Goetz's shoes.[32] The high court wrote and the trial judge spoke in vain. In their deliberations the jury applied a subjective test—Goetz's own test—of whether he faced an imminent danger. He was acquitted of attempted murder and assault but convicted of illegally carrying a gun. Goetz was sentenced to six months in jail, a small fine, and four-and-a-half years probation. After the sentencing a black leader asked, rhetorically, what the verdict and sentence would have been if a black man had attempted summarily to execute four white youths who had approached him in a subway car. A good question.[33]

NONCONFRONTATIONAL KILLINGS

The issue becomes somewhat more complicated when a person kills another absent any violent or threatening confrontation. In North Dakota Janice Leidholm took a butcher knife and stabbed her sleeping husband to death. She had been married to Chester for ten years, during which time he had alternated between drunken violence and sober kindness. On August 6, 1981, they both got drunk at a party, and an argument started. When she tried to call the sheriff, he repeatedly pushed her to the floor. In time Chester fell asleep on their bed. Janice went to the kitchen, got a butcher knife, and stabbed him. The North Dakota jury, applying the reasonable person standard, said that Janice could not have had a reasonable fear of death or serious injury and so convicted her of manslaughter. The judge sentenced her to five years in prison but suspended all but two. Obviously, her history of abuse had elicited sympathy from the court. Despite this leniency, the state supreme court reversed the conviction because the trial judge had failed to tell the jury correctly what a "reasonable person" is. He had defined her "objectively"—that is, as an ordinarily reasonable, cautious, and prudent person. The supreme court held that the standard should be "subjective"—that is, based on the perspective of the defendant. Janice's fear should be judged from Janice's point of view, taking into account her history and experiences, and so the judge should have told the jury to put itself in Janice's shoes and see Chester the way she saw him. Presumably, if a jury so instructed found Janice's fears to be reasonable, she would have to be acquitted on grounds of self-defense.[34]

The Leidholm decision, and some similar cases elsewhere,[35] now provide a wholly new set of rules for judging claims of self-defense: in contrast to the traditional criterion of "objectivity"—that is, what a reasonable person would have believed about the need to defend herself—courts that follow Leidholm can now allow the defendant to claim that her beliefs were reasonable according to a subjective standard—namely, her own beliefs at the time she killed someone. The person defending herself now becomes, in the eyes of the North Dakota and other states, the source of her own exculpatory evidence. And if this is the case, who is to say that killing your oppressor requires even asserting that there is an imminent threat?

But there are legitimate cases in which an abused woman

is so threatened that killing a sleeping husband may seem her only way out. In North Carolina Judy Norman did this to a man who had repeatedly abused her during a twenty-five-year marriage. The day before the shooting, she called the sheriff, but the deputies advised her to file a complaint and left. They returned within an hour when she tried to kill herself with poison. After getting her stomach pumped out, she told her mother she was going to have her husband committed to a mental hospital; he became abusive again. She went to the welfare office to obtain benefits, but John followed her and subjected her to more beatings. That night he made her sleep on the floor. After he dozed off, she got a pistol and killed him.

She was convicted of manslaughter and sentenced to six years in prison. Her appeal to the North Carolina Supreme Court was unavailing. It held that since there was no imme-diate threat to her—he was sleeping—she could not claim self-defense, whether perfect or imperfect. The governor, however, commuted her sentence to time served, and she was out of prison after only two months.[36]

Some scholars have argued that a person in Mrs. Norman's predicament should be able to claim that when it is necessary for a person to kill in self-defense, the concept of necessity should supersede that of immediacy. If you are kidnapped and told that your death will occur in five days, you ought to have the right to kill the kidnapper on the first day even though your death is not yet imminent.[37]

Even though in many states kidnapping is a forcible and atrocious crime that would empower the victim to kill the captor at any time he or she had the chance, there remains the difficult problem of women dependent upon an abusive man. But any effort to allow a claim of mere necessity would open the door to people stretching—as many here described have stretched—the concept of necessity so that a persuasive case that is the basis of the rule soon becomes, through the force of precedent, the grounds for making an objectionable defense in an entirely different case.

Even before the decision in Norman's case, an effort was made in at least two cases to reduce the penalty of women who had hired killers to assassinate their husbands. Both wives claimed, perhaps rightly, to have been abused by their husbands. By not awaiting an imminent threat—by, in effect, taking advantage of the claim that their husbands' deaths were "necessary"—each woman arranged and paid for their husband's execution. In Tennessee, the appeals court had no trouble in reversing the woman's claim that she had acted in "self-defense."[38]

In Missouri, the appellate court had to handle the defense claim that Helen Martin, who had hired a man to kill her husband, Ronald, had not benefited from testimony about her being a battered woman. Dr. Leonore Walker and a psychiatrist, Dr. Wayne Stillings, had been denied an opportunity to prove that out of necessity Helen had the right to purchase her husband's death. Dr. Walker noted that Helen had admitted arranging her husband's death with the killer. That is just what the jury found on the basis of evidence that Helen had hired an assassin, urged him to "hit him again" after he had already shot Ronald once, got a friend to help her clean up the blood, and then had a party that night with the killer and her friend. They found her guilty of murder and the judge gave her fifty years in prison without parole. Given these facts, how could Dr. Walker feel that the jury ought to have heard that Helen was battered? Dr. Walker later explained that living in Helen's town for a while gave her a "dismal, gut-level feeling that I was some-how in danger," that "organized crime" was active in the town, and made her worry that her car would be bombed.[39] Perhaps, perhaps not. But however spooky Hillsboro, Missouri, might have seemed, it is hard to see how the con-sequences of planning a hired murder should be reduced because the victim had been abused. The Missouri court agreed.[40]

A defense based on necessity obviously must have some boundaries or cases like Helen Martin's will in the future be used to authorize private, paid executions. And where necessity seems in fact to be a legitimate and pressing need, as it was for Judy Norman, a gubernatorial pardon or the mild (by North Carolina standards) penalty of the original sentence may ultimately prove the best route.

FROM BATTERED WOMEN TO BATTERED PERSONS

It would be difficult to cite or imagine a criminal defense that is applicable solely to a female defendant. Ordinary fair play, to say nothing of the equal protection clause of the Constitution, suggests that a defense available to one sex be available to both. In February 1989 Paul Kacsmar killed his brother, Francis. At his trial he claimed he acted in self-defense. Paul, a man in his forties, lived with his mother and brother in Pittsburgh. Paul was ill (he had suffered a stroke) and a somewhat wimpy fellow; Francis was a com-bat veteran of Vietnam who liked to practice judo. They did not get along. Francis thought of himself as the head of the house; Paul resented his claims. There were many argu-ments over the years and a few fights. Most of the fights involved pushing and shoving, but sometimes punches were thrown, usually by Francis. Paul denied ever being the aggressor and claimed that Francis sometimes threatened to "beat the hell out of" him. On the night of the shooting, Francis changed the channel on the TV set Paul was watching. Francis accused Paul of not doing his share of the housework. The argument escalated, and Francis hit Paul a few times with his fist. After Paul broke free, he ran to his room, picked up a gun, came back downstairs, and without warning shot the unarmed Francis five times.

Paul was convicted of voluntary manslaughter and sentenced to five to ten years in prison. On appeal a Pennsylvania superior court reversed his conviction on the grounds that the trial judge had not admitted expert testimony that Paul suffered from "battered person syndrome."[41] The court reasoned that if a woman could suffer from battered woman syndrome, a man could suffer from battered person syndrome. The Pennsylvania court repeated the erroneous cliché that expert testimony on such syndromes can dispel the "myths" that abused people are "masochists who are responsible for the abuse." It did not explain who held such a myth or why anyone would suppose that Kacsmar's jury had entertained it.

LAW, SOCIETY, AND ADVOCACY

When the cases of Gladys Kelly, Judy Norman, and Paul Kacsmar came to the attention of appellate judges cognizant of the problem of abuse, they had two choices: they could reassert the traditional law of self-defense and remind lawyers and trial judges that there were ample ways for getting such a defense to the jury and clarifying for them the distinctions between justification, excuse, and mitigation;

or they could help invent a new standard of personal accountability based on poor social science research and dubious theorizing and commend it to trial judges and jurors without clarifying its relationship to the law of self-defense or foreseeing its capacity for protean growth and transformation.

They chose the latter course. By itself this change might have had little effect but for the willingness of many jurors to judge the motives as well as the actions of defendants. Juries will judge the moral worthiness of victims despite the fact that the law rests on the proposition that, except for certain conditions (for example, the victim was trying to kill his killer), all lives are of equal moral worth. Ordinary people have complex views of moral worth and, accordingly, of justice. They will often weigh the motives and character of both victims and defendants and adjust their verdicts accordingly; in extreme cases they will engage in what legal scholars call jury nullification by acquitting a defendant despite overwhelming evidence of guilt. Our sympathy for some defendants—for example, the young Sociz Junatanov—may lead us to feel that the jury's refusal to convict despite conclusive evidence is a sign of its humanity. But a jury that is free to acquit a guilty but likable defendant is also free to convict an innocent but detestable one. For many years southern juries did just that when they refused to convict whites for lynching blacks.

The reason that the criminal law rests on the principle that all lives are valuable and good motives do not (save in cases of self-defense) annul guilt is that it restrains our natural desire to sympathize with people we like (who often turn out to be people like us) and to condemn those we don't like. In the first Menendez trial jurors who have spoken out said they found the story told by the brothers moving and compelling.[42] This not surprising, given the long statements by the accused and their sympathizers portraying the alleged parental mistreatment. Nor is it unprecedented: in 1924 Clarence Darrow blamed the parents of Leopold and Loeb for warping their children's minds so they would kill an innocent boy. When Richard Herrin hammered his girlfriend, Bonnie Garland, to death, Herrin's lawyer succeeded in blaming her for having manipulated him. When a man stabbed his wife to death, his lawyer made the victim out to be a nagging shrew and won him an acquittal based on "temporary insanity."[43] Our legal system does not supply equally talented counsel to poor persons who have also kidnapped, hammered, or stabbed their victims.

Justice is a difficult ideal, vulnerable to attack by benevolence on one side and vengeance on the other. To the extent that the criminal courts allow victims to be put on trial, they foster this siege and allow an affluent defendant to introduce expert witnesses and other evidence that engages the sympathies of jurors while debasing his standards of conduct. The law is, or ought to be, a tough master that by holding us all to a high standard of personal accountability, produces the behavior we wish to see and reduces the opportunity for privilege to corrupt the system.

4
Changing Conceptions of Responsibilty

Often demands are heard that more be done to explain—and thus to mitigate—the penalties to which a defendant is liable. Such demands—which arise not from odd bits of new biological or social science but from a desire to reconcile traditional legal doctrines to evolving social claims—have promoted acceptance of the idea that similar human actions can entail varying degrees of culpability and concomitant differences in legal consequences. This notion is largely the result of three desires: to moderate the severity of legal sanctions, to incorporate the scientific concept of causation, and to use the law to reduce social inequality.

OUR ENGLISH ORIGIN

American criminal law began in England, and it is in England that its evolution has been most closely studied. The popular conception is that until recently the English were savage defenders of the gallows, prescribing hanging for every serious crime and many trivial ones. But recent scholarship has cast considerable doubt on that view by showing that what the English did was often quite different from what they said they would do. Early on English law recognized, in practice if not in writing, the difference between a willful and an accidental act. Though hanging was the standard penalty for most felonies, and certainly for every murder, English juries managed to avoid that result in most cases. Professor Thomas Andrew Green has found that during the medieval period (or at least that part for which written records can be found) the "great majority" of defendants charged with homicide were acquitted.[1] The reason, quite simply, was that every convicted murderer would be executed. Though errors in prosecution were not uncommon, the central fact seems to have been the determination of juries to reserve their guilty verdicts for the few killers who deserved to die. The only lawful device by which the hangman was avoided was the royal pardon. The king had the sovereign right to decide who among the guilty would die and who would be spared. This forced juries to choose between acquitting a defendant and thereby condoning a crime, or convicting him or her and hoping the Crown would supply a pardon. Sometimes the pardon route was tried, but more often an acquittal was chosen.

There was a third alternative available to some defendants. They could avoid the gallows by claiming "benefit of clergy"—that is, by successfully getting their case transferred into the somewhat gentler hands of the church. Becoming a cleric for the purposes of obtaining an ecclesiastical rather than a secular trial sometimes required little more than a demonstration that one could read, and on occasion defendants were allowed to recite a memorized bit of text as proof that they were literate.[2] This system was not only subject to abuse, but it also lacked any sensible rule on which distinctions might be based.

As late as 1660 an English jury was restricted to either ordering a convicted felon hanged or returning him to the community with a brand on his thumb.[3] For lesser offenses the man might be whipped. By 1800, however, new sanctions had been designed. One was incarceration in a prison, the other transportation to a distant colony. J. M. Beattie, who has carefully traced trials during this period, notes that these awkward choices did not become serious ones so long as the crime rate was relatively low, as it was in the villages and small towns of England until late in the eighteenth century. In London, of course, things were different as a growing population made crime more common, and it was there that reliance on imprisonment and transportation was especially common.

All this began to change when the American Revolution reduced the opportunity for transportation and postwar crime rates began to rise. With crime more common and fewer places to which criminals could be shipped, people had to take seriously the effectiveness of the death sentence. When they did, they began to find it both odious and ineffective. A parliamentary commission heard middle-class Londoners testify that with execution the penalty for countless crimes, they were unwilling to bring charges against shoplifters and thieving servants.[4] The general view of crime had changed. It was now seen not as the product of a few odd individuals but of a criminal class whose members were undeterred by executions; indeed, a public that watches a hanging has its own wickedness increased.[5]

The growing belief that the criminal justice system relied excessively on execution began to provide support in the early nineteenth century for the creation of a uniformed police force and the adoption of a series of legal changes.

But reform in those days meant something very different from what it came to mean at the end of the century. Professor Martin J. Wiener has shown that the crime wave that struck England in the 1820s and 1830s was met by moderating penalties (the death penalty was abolished for all offenses save murder and treason) but making those that remained more certain.[6] The number of hangings declined, public hangings were abolished, and the movement against capital punishment steadily gained strength. All of these changes lightened the burden on unguided jurors. But at the same time the reach of the criminal law was lengthened, the range of acceptable excuses narrowed. Vagrants, drunkards, prostitutes, and disorderly juveniles were systematically made subject to legal penalties, now more easily enforced with the creation of a professional police force.[7] Prosecution was made easier, punishment more certain, and penalties more predictable. "The guiding vision of this reconstructed system of criminal justice," Wiener has written, "was that of the responsible individual."[8] The criminal law was increasingly expected to hold people accountable: "A crucial supposition underlying early Victorian attempts at law reform was that the most desirable way of making people self-governing was to hold them, sternly and unblinkingly, responsible for the consequences of their actions."[9]

This belief helps explain why the British were inclined to link milder penalties with greater self-governance. They were reluctant to accept the idea that crimes were the result of recklessness or negligence. Such a view, if adopted, would encourage people to underinvest in foreseeing the likely results of their actions and would thereby weaken the support the law gave to the creation of self-governing people. Not only were the British slow to accept the idea of excuses, but they also kept in place rules that made it difficult to ascertain the mental state on which such excuses would depend. There was no clearly stated insanity defense until 1843. Before 1853 defendants were not allowed to testify at their own trials; it was not until 1898 that they were allowed to testify under oath.

The desire to maintain a system of moderate but extensive penalties was strengthened by the establishment of a modern police force so that the greater certainty of the law might replace the unconstrained choices of juries. This was no easy task, for many people feared that a police force meant an increase in national executive authority. But Sir Robert Peel managed to create the uniformed English bobby in a way that produced growing acceptance of what once was widely rejected. That the police would supervise the public made it easier to weaken the awesome (though infrequently imposed) threat of execution. New, lesser penalties were put in place that permitted jurors to avoid the old system of acquitting guilty men in order to avoid the gallows.

The early Victorian attitude toward crime changed profoundly during the second half of the nineteenth century. The early Victorians wished to hold man responsible and so viewed him as choosing between crime and duty; to them the central problem was to deal with a fallible human nature that too easily gave way to lust, greed, and impulsiveness. By the end of Victoria's reign, however, the crime rate was declining, and this atmosphere of relative social peace seemed conducive to the view that crime resulted more from social injustices than personal failings. Accordingly, England began to broaden the range of excuses and make punishment less certain; as crime rates declined, prison sentences grew shorter.[10] The English had come to think that a people were not entirely responsible for their actions, that crime was socially caused and not personally chosen, and that human nature was good when it had not been corrupted by society, illness, or genetic defect.

But if the existence of social peace made possible a causal theory of crime, the rise of science made it inevitable. In part it was a matter of modern science eclipsing revealed religion within the minds of intellectual and political elites. The self-control impulse of the early nineteenth century had been compatible with and was reinforced by evangelical teachings that stressed the weakness of the human spirit and the need to restrain human appetites. As Wiener has pointed out, religion and utilitarianism, though fundamentally at odds, had enlisted in the same cause: to induce people to assign a higher weight to the more distant consequences of their actions. Jeremy Bentham, James Mill, and others wrote frequently of the need to design legal codes and political arrangements that would make shortsighted people more farsighted and thus more prudent. Victorian preachers had much the same goal, though to achieve it they employed the prospect of eternal more than earthly punishment.[11]

Some critics of the character-building enterprise of the early Victorians dismiss it as a way of advancing upper-class interests against the poor. There was an element of class perspective in this, to be sure, but it was really not an "interest," and its object was to achieve something that most people of any class cherished—getting men to behave responsibly, which is to say, getting them to stop stealing, rioting, drinking, gambling, fornicating, and dueling. A few historians may think that this wickedness was so concentrated among the poor that controlling it was equivalent to subjugating them, but in fact many of these evils—especially drinking, gambling, fornicating, and dueling—were the pastimes of the idle aristocracy. There is little doubt that both the utilitarians and the evangelicals were interested in curbing aristocratic as well as popular excesses.

By the early twentieth century, however, utilitarianism and religion had lost much of their appeal to the upper middle classes. These philosophical impulses were too earnest, too self-righteous, too confining (too repressive, Freud was later to say); they took the fun out of life.[12] Through self-expression restless individuals sought to liberate themselves from the dogged discipline of consequences.

Moreover, science did not simply question religion, it made an argument against it. That argument was both biomedical and environmental. Current critics of genetic and medical theories of crime would do well to recall that the leading British advocates of these views, including many now viewed as monstrous by contemporary environmentalists, were reformers who wished to excuse criminals as the victims of their own heritage. Charles Goring, though he refuted Cesare Lombroso's crude theory of criminal atavism, nonetheless found physical and intellectual differences between convicts and noncriminals. The law, he felt, should take these differences into account. Cyril Burt, famous for his studies of the heritability of intelligence, argued that juvenile delinquency was the result of "misdirected energy" that could not be stamped out but might be redirected through appropriate social programs. Goring, Burt, and others believed that criminals differ only in degree from noncriminals, and much of that difference is the result of factors—age, genetic inheritance, social circumstance— over which the offender has little control.[13]

The loosening of the criminal law and the rise of a therapeutic ethic could not proceed in a political vacuum. When England abolished the death penalty for murder in 1965, it left in its place a mandatory sentence of life imprisonment. That outcome, necessary politically, confronted those who wished to moderate penalties even further with a continuing problem. The 1957 Homicide Act stated that an unlawful killing would be regarded as manslaughter rather than murder if the killer was provoked so that he lost his self-control or if the killer suffered from some abnormality of the mind that substantially impaired his mental responsibility.[14] A judge can render any sentence he wishes to a person convicted of manslaughter.

These two exceptions to a murder conviction have since become the rule rather than the exception. In 1990 the English police arrested 556 persons on charges of homicide; of these, 80 were acquitted and 46 dropped away owing to suicide or insanity. Of the 428 that remained and were convicted of an offense, over half were found guilty of manslaughter.[15] Every English jurist to whom one speaks immediately agrees that the defenses provided by the Homicide Act—provocation and diminished responsibility—are used largely in order to avoid the mandatory life sentence for murder.

But the changes were not limited to homicide or minimizing life imprisonment. Various English scholars have observed that the likelihood of prison following upon the commission of almost any crime dropped substantially during the very time when crime rates were rising. Between 1984 and 1992 the number of robberies more than doubled, but the number of persons sent to prison for robbery went up only slightly (by less than one quarter).[16] One study found that in the early 1950s about 25 percent of offenders were sentenced to prison. By the mid–1970s only one in ten met that fate.[17] To check against the possibility that this decline in the use of prison was due to an increase in less serious offenses, the authors looked at particular crimes, notably theft, burglary, and violence against a person. There was a general decline in the use of prison for those convicted of these crimes.[18]

David P. Farrington and Patrick A. Langan examined the same problem from a slightly different perspective. By using data from the British Crime Survey (a study of how many times individual victims suffered from crime whether or not they called the police), they concluded that the number of offenses committed by burglars or auto thieves increased markedly in the 1980s. In 1987 the average burglar or auto thief had to commit twice as many crimes as his 1981 counterpart in order to receive a prison sentence.[19]

THE AMERICAN EXPERIENCE

We have no history of American criminal justice quite comparable to what Green, Beattie, Wiener, and others have chronicled for England, but the available studies suggest the same nineteenth-century concern for using the law to enhance self-control. Laws against public disorder and indecency were strengthened at the same time that the death penalty and other severe penalties were becoming less common.[20]

But in the twentieth century America's reaction to rising crime rates was very different from that of England. At the beginning of the great crime increase that started in the early 1960s, the American judiciary had been reducing the number of offenders sent to prison. Despite mounting crime rates, the inmates of state prisons dropped from 213,000 in 1960 to 196,000 in 1970.[21] But as crime continued to rise, the criminal justice system changed its response. Prison populations began to rise dramatically, an increase that continued in the 1980s and early 1990s despite the fact that, according to the victimization studies conducted by the Census Bureau, the rate of most forms of crime was declining. Between 1970 and 1990, the number of inmates more than tripled; between 1990 and 1993, the increase was over 20 percent.[22]

These swelling numbers were not due to an increase in the average time served, which dropped sharply for most offenses between 1950 and 1990. Nor did the rise in drug offenses make much difference before around 1986; until that time, when crack cocaine became a major object of law enforcement efforts, drug offenders made up no more than about 8 percent of all inmates. What really made the difference in imprisonment was an increased willingness of prosecutors and judges to send those convicted of crime to prison.[23]

ENGLAND VERSUS AMERICA

Though Americans cut the time served by the average prison inmate, they increased the chances of going to prison. This was the opposite of the British experience. How do we account for two legal systems, largely identical in the eighteenth century, having such a dramatically different response to crime in the late twentieth century? This puzzle is magnified by the fact that not only did both nations have rising crime rates (rises that continued much longer in England than in America), but they also had voters who were deeply upset about crime and (during the 1980s) conservative national political regimes.

There are clear signs that the English policy reflected the views of the government. In 1985 the Home Office instructed all local police forces to warn (in English parlance, caution) juvenile offenders instead of arresting them. During almost the entire period of rising British crime rates, the senior staff of the Home Office was preoccupied with reducing, or at least minimizing, the British prison population.[24] In part this reflected a desire to reduce costs and prevent overcrowding, but in part it also reflected a belief that imprisonment was the wrong way to deal with most offenders. In pursuit of these goals, the Home Office decreased the minimum time required for parole eligibility and the granting of parole became nearly automatic.

At the same time Parliament made its views clear. In 1991 it adopted a Criminal Justice Act that restricted the imposition of custodial sentences. Each court was instructed that it should "not pass a custodial sentence on the offender unless it is of the opinion that the offense . . . was so serious that only such a sentence can be justified for the offense." It excepted from this restriction "violent or sexual" offenses that require custody "adequate to protect the public from serious harm. . . ."[25] A court later interpreted this injunction to mean that custody was required only when "all right-thinking members of the public, knowing all the facts, feel that justice would not be done" by anything less.[26] The clear lesson was to avoid prison except where essential.

It is hard to imagine a similar response occurring in America. We know that during the 1960s the prison population declined while crime was increasing, but very soon a reaction set in. Throughout the 1970s and 1980s American public opinion redirected American penal policy, leading to a sharp increase in the chances that a convicted offender would go to prison. Most states passed mandatory sentencing laws for repeat and serious offenders, and these rules may have had some effect on the number of prison inmates.

The differences in response to crime arose despite the presence of Margaret Thatcher at 10 Downing Street and Ronald Reagan in the White House. This suggests how fundamentally different are the American and British political systems. The central difference, I think, is that the gap between public opinion and official governance is wider in England than in America. You will not notice this gap if you confine your knowledge of our British cousins to the contents of their daily newspapers. Every day these publications are devoted to advancing some version of the radical equality of all men by exploiting the travails of the royal family, attacking the opinions of elected officials, or denouncing the advantages of business leaders. The leader of the Labour Party has called for removing hereditary lords from the House of Lords, a proposition generally defended by the press. The noisy commotion of a parliamentary session and the riotous tumult of English soccer fans, whether at home or abroad, are legendary, both suggesting a kind of shared commitment to doing your own thing as vigorously and as rudely as possible.

But behind this public display of egalitarianism there lives an ancient system of authority in which hierarchy, power, and central management are alive and well. English criminal courts are managed by judges wearing elaborate robes and wigs who often intervene in a trial to guide testimony, summarize evidence, and instruct the jury. Prosecution and defense counsel, also wearing robes and wigs, are much less likely than their American counterparts to offer objections or make appeals. English judges must refuse to allow an appeal from a criminal trial if they decide that no actual miscarriage of justice occurred.[27] (The much greater frequency of appeals in American criminal trials has been evident since the early days of this century.[28]) English defense counsel does not sit with the accused (he or she is kept in a separate dock) and may be chosen from the same barristers' chambers that has supplied the prosecutor. Luncheon for the judges at the Central Criminal Courts in London is an elaborate affair supplied by the sheriff (also dressed in robes), who supplies wines and elegant service. As one barrister remarked, the central fact of English criminal trials is the powerful display of centralized authority.

These traditional flourishes notwithstanding, the system is not obviously biased against the defendant. In 1994, for example, about two-thirds of all criminal defendants pled guilty (a lower proportion than one would find in most American courts). Of those who pled not guilty, more than half were acquitted by either the judge's ruling or the decision of the jury.[29]

The true lesson of the English system is not that it favors or penalizes the defendant but that it favors the regime. It does so by taking full advantage of the English tendency to defer to authority. The judges are selected by the lord chancellor; there are no elections. The chancellor's functions recognize no doctrine of separated powers: he sits in the cabinet (and so is in the executive branch); he presides over the judiciary (and so is in the judicial branch); and he serves as speaker of the House of Lords (and so is in the legislative branch). His duties are vast. By heading the judiciary, he runs a department with twelve thousand members.[30] The

British civil service is more remote from—and can act more liberally than—their American counterparts.

The prime minister governs the state during his or her five-year term with assured knowledge that whatever he or she proposes to the House of Commons will be adopted (after, of course, a good deal of noisy opposition challenges). Criminal justice policy is largely in the hands of the home secretary. Unless the prime minister feels strongly that crime is a major electoral problem, he or she has no incentive to appoint a home secretary (or a lord chancellor) who will defer to public opinion.

This system of concentrated authority permits the English government to take bold steps but at the price of only consulting itself and its elite advisers as to what steps are bold. In the United States, by contrast, authority is so widely distributed that rarely can anyone take a bold—or sometimes even a small—step. The virtue of this defect is that it amplifies the demands of the public. When power is in countless independent hands, all dependent on public opinion, each hand responds to the constituencies to which it is attuned. The collective force of strong popular feelings may be clumsy or inconsistent, but it is powerful. When Americans want prosecutors or courts to be tougher, they generally get tougher.

The English political system empowers a government; our system empowers voices that claim to speak for the people. Since the presidential election of 1964, American voices have urged a tougher stance on crime. During that same time English voices with the same message were not heard until quite recently. In May 1993 Prime Minister John Major appointed Michael Howard as home secretary. He set about trying to toughen English criminal laws and court procedures by requiring longer minimum sentences (by mid-1996 not yet achieved), a reduction in parole, and some restrictions on the ability of defendants to conceal their prior criminal record from juries. These initiatives immediately earned him the enmity of the lord chief justice, Lord Taylor, and many judges, to say nothing of most members of what the British call their "chattering classes." The leading newspapers were generally highly critical of Howard's proposals. It is a quarrel that has many counterparts in the United States, but with one large difference: here the local equivalents of Mr. Howard would have spoken out two decades earlier, and their views would generally have prevailed with much less effective opposition.

ANGLO-AMERICAN LEGAL DOCTRINE

From the late nineteenth century to the present, legal doctrine in England and America has changed dramatically. In both nations elite opinion, often bolstered by public views, sought ways to further moderate state control of private action. What had once been a crime—for example, vagrancy or public drunkenness—became in many places a status, and as such immunized the perpetrator from arrest or prosecution. In many cities people who would have been arrested if they slept in public places were now escorted to public places where they were encouraged to sleep. Beggars who once risked arrest for soliciting passersby were now sent to public feeding stations financed by the taxpayer.

These changes were examples of a broader alteration in opinions as to what constituted human nature and how the law should inform that nature. These alterations have produced the inevitable public reaction, one that reaffirms deterrence and retribution as the basis for punishment and urges that vagrancy be reduced, begging curtailed, public drunks arrested, and some juveniles treated as adults. The social importance (and, I should add, the political popularity) of deterrence has put defenders of individualized justice and criminal rehabilitation on the defensive. But it has not, I think, done much to check the tendency to elaborate a more general and inclusive theory of excuses (or mitigation) based on the notion that since crime is socially caused, personal responsibility is diminished.

Reinforcing this tendency has been the desire to recognize within the criminal justice system the existence of social inequality and to use trials (or pleas) as a way of reducing that inequality—or at least what are taken to be its effects. This use was already evident by the turn of the century. The legal instruments of society should try to set right the byproducts of indifference or social oppression. If one examines the long list of factors, both hereditary and environmental, that increase the likelihood of criminal behavior, one is struck, I think, by the growing tendency of judges to validate those factors that embody the claims of the putatively disadvantaged defendant. We wish to help veterans suffering from posttraumatic stress disorder or wives systematically abused by their husbands, but we are much less moved by the claims of men suffering from high levels of testosterone, low levels of manganese, minor physical anomalies, inadequate schooling, or low verbal intelligence. A woman suffering from prementsrual syndrome may get some special advantage, but a man beset by his hormonal deficiencies will get less.

The instrument most often used as the correctional device is the doctrine of diminished capacity or diminished responsibility. The doctrine holds that the defendant, although not insane, was suffering from a mental condition that either prevented him from intentionally breaking the law or reduced the extent to which he ought to be held fully accountable for his action. His responsibility can be diminished by a mental disease, mental retardation, intoxication, or other conditions. If the doctrine is used to show that a person did not intend to commit a crime, then it is no different from any other defense designed to show the absence of a guilty mind. For example, if it can be shown that a man who killed another man did not plan the killing, then the defendant in most states would not be guilty of premeditated murder. But the doctrine can also be used to assert that, though the defendant intended to commit the crime, he is only partially responsible for that decision. Other factors share in that responsibility. In 1988 the English Privy Council did away with the requirement that a defendant's belief in the need to defend himself by killing another be objectively reasonable. Lord Lane, speaking for the Council, abolished the reasonableness requirement that had governed since time immemorial and substituted a mere requirement of honesty: "If the belief was in fact held, its unreasonableness . . . is neither here nor there. It is irrelevant."[31] This change in English law is a bold one, and carries matters much further than they have yet moved in this country.

American criminal justice has been driven to a greater degree than its English counterpart by popular demands that penalties become tougher and convictions more common. But the American and English system are alike in the extent to which, without much public notice, judges and legislators broaden those circumstances under which defendants can claim excusing or mitigating conditions. The result has been a system that, in the United States, attaches much higher maximum penalties to many crimes but in fact only imposes the maximum in rare cases.

By modifying the criminal law—in large measure that of homicide, but other laws as well—so as to acknowledge social causation, we risk taking a principle (the need to assess the guilt or innocence of an accused person) and modify it with a preference (intoxication or diminished capacity or personal battering) that moderates the penalty for people suffering from an unsupported list of partial excuses.

Among the several ways in which a principle differs from a preference is our belief that the former ought to govern our actions even when the actions we take are unappetizing, the people they benefit unattractive, and the consequences for us unpleasant. This is not to say that following the dictates of principle—that is, doing our duty—is always obnoxious; there are many duties that we do with pleasure and many principles we obey with delight. But if the only principles we follow are ones that direct us to do nice things to attractive people, we are likely to suspect that many of these rules are not really principles at all.

The introduction of excuses and mitigations into the English and American criminal law was driven in part by our enlarged sympathies for people who faced torture and death. As more people objected to capital and corporal punishment, more people agreed to accept excuses for those accused of offenses that entailed such penalties. These excuses have been chiefly reserved for homicide—partly because homicide was the offense most likely to result in a gruesome penalty and partly because it is hard to imagine how anyone might rob or rape another "negligently."

Despite their great differences, English and American courts have moved together to embrace a wider array of excuses and mitigations as a reflection of the view of judges and experts that this acceptance is required by the lessons of social science and the dictates of social justice.

5
Law and Responsibility

Contrary to what many suppose, there is no avalanche of "abuse excuses" afflicting American criminal law. There are many cases in which such excuses are raised and a few in which they may seem to have been granted, though the absence of any systematic study of trial court behavior makes even that judgment suspect. And, of course, there are countless law review articles urging such excuses. But appellate court opinions and statutory law do not, in general, conform to the expectations raised by some cases and many essays.

Though no avalanche has occurred, the courts are having difficulty keeping their footing on a slope that has become increasingly slippery. Over many years, judges have been alert to certain claims presented by defendants who suffer from conditions that seem to demand sympathy. When the condition has acquired the status of a socially defined problem rather than the claim of an unattractive defendant, a judge will yield ground. And when one does that, many follow—whether or not the condition explains the crime. As other judges follow suit, the door is opened wide to expert testimony designed to explain criminal actions in ways that will lead juries to excuse the act or mitigate the punishment.

I have outlined this tendency in three respects: imperfect self-defense, personal intoxication, and battered women, considering each from two perspectives—judging the defendant and explaining the defendant's actions. When a jury *judges* a defendant, it considers his or her mental state only to the extent necessary to establish the existence of one or another of a small list of excusing or justifying defenses, such as insanity, necessity, or self-defense. But when a jury *explains* the defendant's actions, it searches for a full account of the factors—the motives, circumstances, and beliefs— that caused them.

To understand the difference, compare how most people feel about crime when they are citizens with how they feel when a juror. As citizens they denounce crime and urge greater severity to reduce it, but as jurors they seek to explain the crime and link penalties to those explanations. Thirty years ago Harry Kalven and Hans Zeisel compared how judges and juries evaluated cases. Usually they agreed, but when they did not the judges were more severe than the jurors.[1]

Recently, Norman J. Finkel published an extensive study of experimental research on juries that reveals how the juror's desire for explanation often overrides the citizen's desire for punishment. In one case Finkel asked experimental jurors to penalize a man for writing a hundred-dollar check against an imaginary bank account. As he repeated the test, he added facts for and against the defendant. When the jurors heard he had a long criminal record, the penalty they endorsed went up from ten months to thirty years. When they heard a psychiatrist testify for the defendant, the penalty fell from thirty to five years; when they heard one psychiatrist testify for the defendant and another for the prosecution, the penalty settled at fifteen years.[2]

Similarly, when experimental jurors heard the case of a battered woman who killed her abusive husband under three different conditions—she was a good wife and mother, she was an incompetent wife and mother, she was a bad wife and mother—the percentage of guilty verdicts rose dramatically as the woman went from the good-wife to the bad-wife end of the scale, even though her goodness or badness had, legally, nothing to do with the rightness of her actions.[3]

IMPERFECT SELF-DEFENSE

The two trials of Erik and Lyle Menendez illustrate the difficulty courts face in managing the relationship between the jury's obligation to judge a case and its desire to explain it. When the Menendez brothers were first tried, Judge Stanley Weisberg was evidently uncomfortable with defense demands that the jury hear all manner of evidence designed to discredit the two dead victims, yet he allowed much of it to be presented. A central reason was the agreement by the prosecution that the brothers were entitled to advance the claim of imperfect self-defense; the claim, that is, that they killed their parents out of an "honest though unreasonable belief" that their own lives were in danger. The jury heard from six psychiatrists who had treated the dead mother for drug usage and depression or who supported the brothers' claim of psychosexual abuse, as well as from Lyle Menendez and many friends and teachers about the brothers' entire family history. Had the judge exerted his powers under California law, he might have excluded much of it. But he did not.

The California Evidence Code empowers judges to exclude evidence if its "probative value"—that is, its tendency to prove a claim—is substantially outweighed by the probability that its admission will either consume an "undue" amount of time or "create a substantial danger of undue prejudice, of confusing the issues, or of misleading the jury."[4] These provisions would seemingly allow the judge to control a criminal trial, especially since it is the announced rule of appellate courts that they will only reluctantly reverse a judge on the evidence he allows to be heard. Moreover, when Judge Weisberg was a prosecutor, he had sought a first-degree murder conviction against a son who had killed his wealthy father under circumstances similar to those of the Menendez case.

But the judge's experience and the Evidence Code rulings were of little value in a court system in which murder convictions are regularly appealed and appeals courts routinely issue new instructions. The appellate process no doubt protects our rights, but it also reinforces the lawyers' desire to press for the admission of evidence and magnifies the extent to which legal reasoning creates unintended consequences.

The prospect of appellate review has thoroughly affected the criminal courts. Judges, prosecutors, and defense counsel are drawn from a culture in which they routinely see most criminal cases ending in negotiated guilty verdicts and a small number of contested cases resulting in appeals. A contested case is one that has become increasingly dominated by lawyers, with every legal issue challenged and judges ruling endlessly on countless efforts to silence or redirect the other party.

This need not be the case, and in fact is not the case in most European courts, including the English ones from which the American legal system took its origins. Here, trials have increasingly grown in length as the search for truth has been subordinated to the manipulation of procedures. In England the average criminal trial in 1982 took only about one day, while in Los Angeles the average one took about five days (up from three days in 1953). The robbery trial of Patty Hearst lasted forty days; the Menendez brothers' first trial took six months and the second one five months; the McMartin School molestation trial took two and a half years.[5]

American trials are long because they are complex; they are complex because every issue is contested; issues are contested because failing to object will weaken each side's chance of success on appeal and expose a defendant's attorney to the objection that he supplied ineffective counsel. In such an atmosphere many judges feel constrained to adopt a defensive mode in which it is better to admit testimony (and thus minimize the chances of a reversal on appeal) than to exclude it and risk such a reversal. A judge is an umpire, but not one like those found in football or basketball, where play is limited by the clock, time-outs are few and closely counted, and many infractions are ignored. Our judges are more like baseball umpires presiding over a game in which the clock plays no role, time-outs are endless, and every play must be called.

The likelihood of appeal in contested criminal cases is due to the nature of legal reasoning. Edward H. Levi, in his brilliant essay *An Introduction to Legal Reasoning,* argues that lawyers reason by example or by analogy. The logic of analogical reasoning is that if two cases are the same in one relevant aspect, they are the same in all relevant aspects.[6] The key issue is whether different cases can be treated as though they were the same. This is, as Levi notes, an imperfect system of reasoning, for it does not depend on deduction—that is, on reasoning from a clear rule to a particular case. A word or phrase found to govern one case is made to apply to later cases that may differ in crucial features. As Judge Benjamin Cardozo suggested of metaphors, a word starts out to free thought and ends by enslaving it.[7]

Levi illustrates the problem with the history of the Mann Act, intended to abolish what was then known as "white slavery." The law, passed in 1910, makes it a federal felony to "knowingly transport" in "interstate commerce" a woman "for the purpose of prostitution or debauchery, or for any other immoral purpose."[8] The courts, trying to give meaning to such ambiguous phrases as "debauchery" and "immoral purpose," extended the scope of the law to make it illegal for a woman to cross a state line voluntarily for purposes of sex, to be moved to an employment where debauchery might occur, to voluntarily accompany the man to whom she was a mistress, or to accompany a vacationing Mormon family that happened to be polygamous.[9]

Much the same modification of a law occurred with respect to the California rule of imperfect self-defense. When the state supreme court established the rule, it did so in a case that involved two violent men with a long history of personal antagonism confronting each other in a parking lot. One man reached for his pocket, possibly for a weapon; the other drew a gun and shot him. The supreme court felt that Flannel may have thought his life was in danger and did not want him to be convicted of murder.[10] To achieve this it said that Flannel may have had an "honest but unreasonable" belief that he needed to defend himself. If so, he should only be convicted of manslaughter.

In the years between the Flannel decision and the Menendez trial, various California appellate courts reviewed cases in which the claim of imperfect self-defense might have been raised. With few exceptions the appeals involved fights, many drunken ones, in which one person killed another. One involved a tussle in a bar, another a street gang fight, and still others various domestic disputes involving flying fists, raging arguments, and angry threats.[11] These cases produced the everyday murders with which the police are routinely involved. All had in common a direct confrontation, infused with imminent violence, between angry and upset people.

The Menendez case was radically different. There was no fight, no struggle, no apparently imminent threat to the lives of the sons. Yet in the first trial the judge allowed the defense to put the dead parents on trial as if there had been such threats and instructed the jury that they could consider the claim that the sons had acted on the basis of imperfect self-defense. Half of the jurors agreed.

Before the second trial began, the California Supreme Court clarified the rule. A boy named Christian shot and killed another man, Robert Elliott, who was a skinhead and gang member. After being physically and verbally assaulted by Elliott's friends, Christian began carrying a gun. One day Elliott chased Christian down the beach, threatening him. Christian turned and fired, killing him. When the trial court ignored Christian's claims of self-defense, the Supreme Court reviewed it.

The Court explained what should have been obvious from

the first: imperfect self-defense is the honest belief in "imminent peril to life or great bodily injury"; when it exists, the crime is no greater than manslaughter. The threat to the defendant "must be instantly dealt with."*[12] This should not have come as a surprise to the attorneys or the judge in the Menendez trial. Before the trial a California appeals court had already ruled, in the case of a woman who had killed her abusive but sleeping husband, that a threat must be "imminent," by which the law means immediate—that is, "must be instantly dealt with."[13] Even in the case of imperfect self-defense, the value the law attaches to human life means that no court would have sentenced the abusive husband to death for a murder he had only threatened to commit; similarly, no woman defending herself can be excused from some finding of guilt because she killed a man whom she believed might kill her in the future.

In the second Menendez trial the prosecution advanced this view and Judge Weisberg relied on it, ruling against a number of defense witnesses and refusing to instruct the jury that they could consider imperfect self-defense. This ruling meant that the jurors now could choose only between murder (in the first or second degree) or acquittal. The jury agreed on first-degree murder convictions.

Much of this legal maneuvering might have been

---

*When the court converted an "imminent" peril into one that must be "instantly" dealt with, it made a mistake. Oliver Wendell Holmes once remarked that detached reflection cannot be demanded in the presence of an uplifted knife. Christian, having shot a threatening youth who had once assaulted him, is now in jail because the court felt he was too quick in firing at a pursuing attacker. I doubt that most people would think that you must let your attacker get within arm's reach before striking back.

avoided if the legislature had acted on the matter. Imperfect self-defense was created by the courts, not by the legislature; indeed, some authorities think that when the California legislature abolished the diminished capacity rule after the Dan White case it meant to abolish imperfect self-defense as well.[14] Whatever the legislature intended, a court-invented criminal defense, designed to spare a person from what judges thought was an overly severe sentence, came close to sparing two persons in totally different circumstances from a comparable penalty.

The danger remains. Consider this: Had Erik and Lyle studied the law, they would have known what to do. First, get in a fight with their parents. The subject would not matter, as long as they were upset. Second, claim that the father advanced toward them, reaching for his pocket. Third, shoot their parents. Finally, plant a gun near the father. Under California law they would surely have been able to claim imperfect self-defense and would have had an excellent chance of being convicted of voluntary manslaughter, for which the penalty can be only three years. With any luck, they might well have been acquitted under the "battered person" rule. Then enjoy the inheritance of several million dollars.

Next time, some rich boy will do exactly this.

INTOXICATION

Until early in the nineteenth century, the general rule in English and American law was that drunkenness is never a defense to a crime.[15] Later in that century the old rule was modified: although intoxication could not excuse a murder, it could reduce the severity of the conviction if the defendant was too drunk to have premeditated the killing.

There are conflicting views on the reasons for this change. One is that in the nineteenth century we began a period in which "criminal liability is to be sharply differentiated from moral delinquency."[16] There is some truth in this; English law during the latter part of the nineteenth century generally began to separate moral fault from a legal fault out of the growing belief that one's moral status was a product of social forces over which one had only modest control. Another view, not inconsistent with the first, is that judges were increasingly looking for ways to moderate the severity of the death sentence for murder by finding mental states that would show a defendant had not acted with malice. This tendency was confirmed in the twentieth century with the growth of a medical theory of alcoholism. The legal theorists who accepted this view inferred that an alcoholic lacks the capacity to control his drinking. An alcoholic takes a drink voluntarily only in the sense that he wills it, but he lacks the power—or so the theory goes—to will otherwise.[17] If the alcoholic "lacks the substantial capacity" to avoid drinking, then what he does while drunk is not a full measure of his moral capacity.

The combined effect of these sentiments was to create, by the beginning of the twentieth century, the view that intoxication could explain away one's intent to commit a crime. Since hardly anyone wanted drunkards excused of any criminal liability no matter what they did, a halfway house had to be established in which intoxication would become a partial excuse. This was done by linking intoxication to the dubious distinction between crimes that reflect a "general" intent and ones that require an additional "specific" intent. If I enter your house unlawfully, I am guilty of breaking and entering, but if I enter it unlawfully with an intent to steal, I am guilty of burglary. The entry reflects general intent, the stealing specific intent. Similarly, assault is a general intent crime, but assault with intent to rape is a specific intent one. Intoxication would not excuse entering the home or committing the assault, but it could excuse the burglary or the attempted rape. But the logic of this view is to assert, without evidence of which I am aware, that an inebriated person who intends to enter someone else's house unlawfully or intends to start a fight with a woman nonetheless lacks the capacity to intend a burglary or to intend a rape. Many persons while drunk can plan an illegal housebreak or start a fight with enough skill to win and afterwards try to avoid arrest or lie to the officers; such people are nonetheless said to be "too drunk" to have intended a theft or a rape.[18] Intoxication as a partial defense is a slippery slope on which the law can find little comfortable purchase.

By the middle of this century, the view that alcoholism was a disease had taken firm root. Jerome Hall gave it a characteristically witty and trenchant explanation in 1944.[19] He derided the rule that voluntary intoxication is no defense against a criminal charge by claiming that this reflects an outmoded "rationalistic psychology" that "ignores the complex psychic apparatus of self-restraint."[20]

In Canada the Supreme Court held that an intoxicated person when interviewed by the police could not give a statement "voluntarily," and so a confession she made at the time—even after having being offered a right to counsel—was invalid.[21] A few years later another Canadian court held that intoxication was a defense against a murder charge and ordered the drunk killer's sentence reduced to manslaughter.[22]

Once again the logic of scientific explanation has crept

back into the law so as to selectively distort the principle of moral agency and legal culpability. Suppose I were not a chronic drunk but instead lacked self-restraint because I was awash in testosterone, afflicted with attention deficit disorder, enmeshed in a constant rage against the evils of the world, and deprived of more than a rudimentary capacity for intelligent conversation. Suppose, in short, I was like a large number of murderers. My lack of self-restraint would be at least as great as that of the chronic drunk, but I would not enjoy their privileged excuse from full culpability. To think otherwise one would be required, I think, to suspend the enforcement of most criminal laws.

Now if as a result of intoxication (or hormonal imbalance or head injury) I was delusional—that is, I acted without knowing right from wrong or up from down—I could plead insanity. But absent that condition, my psychic state—always, to follow Professor Hall, highly "complex"—would have no bearing on my legal culpability. Indeed, intoxication would have even less relevance to my legal standing than my hormonal condition because the former can be changed more easily than the latter, as is evident from the millions of people who participate in Alcoholics Anonymous.

One important reason why people join AA is that neither the moral sense of their fellow citizens nor (ordinarily) their standing before the courts of law grants them much slack. If morality and the law did not enforce an obligation toward reasonable sobriety, there would be much less sobriety and much more crime.[23]

Taking the opposite view, whether by allowing drunkenness as a defense or by creating the fictional distinction between general and specific intent crimes, is simply a way of inventing a doctrine of partial excuse for a common human failing toward which many jurists have acquired, over the last century, a certain personal sympathy.

BATTERED WOMEN

For far too long the courts, like people generally, neglected the problem of battered women. When a realization of the magnitude of the problem was highlighted by popular writings and social movements, the courts felt compelled to act. They did so as the courts often do when they first become aware of a new issue—quickly, magisterially, and inadequately. The first book they read became the definitive treatise (though it was not), and once one court had acted, other courts followed suit by copying its decision with little further reflection.

With little detached scrutiny the courts accepted claims that jurors were biased by myths they allegedly had about battered women and that there existed a cohort of serious scholars who could testify with expert authority about the psychological condition of abused women. Some courts took the view that a real or imaginary threat to a woman had to be judged from the subjective perspective of the killer, not from the traditional viewpoint of a reasonable person.[24] Once this standard is admitted, then anyone, male or female, who can plausibly claim prior abuse can ask the jury to limit his or her penalty to voluntary manslaughter; moreover, it implies the possibility of at least partial extenuation, rare in practice but frightening in prospect, for killing one's abuser when he or she is asleep.

It must be understood that the courts are not well organized to adopt new criminal defenses. Unlike legislatures they do not hold hearings, engage in public debate, or persuade people of diverse political orientations to accept a fresh doctrine. Because they are not legislators, they are not compelled to do more than link a new defense to an existing legal doctrine—that is, to reason by analogy—rather than to design that defense around a complete account of the circumstances in which it might be used.

In California the courts created the doctrine of diminished responsibility to accommodate the problem of a young boy who, though judged to be sane, was clearly disturbed, and as a result killed his mother so that her home would be available to him for planned sexual escapades. Because the court did not want to imprison such a boy for life, it announced that though sane, he was "not a fully normal or mature, mentally well person" and should be guilty of nothing more than second-degree murder.[25] But a new legal doctrine, crafted to extend sympathy to a disturbed young man, became a state judicial rule that then was extended by defense attorneys to all manner of cases, including Dan White's assassination of two San Francisco officials.

Legislators can, of course, make the same mistakes, but they are less likely to do so given their organization (they are large institutions composed of people who disagree) and their public accountability (they fight over these issues in full view of the press). As a result, a new legal rule will generally be fashioned by a legislature with less regard for the needs of a particular defendant and with more regard to full array of cases and circumstances to which the rule will likely apply.

CHANGING THE LAW

Finding the right balance between judgment and explanation is not easily done, but let me suggest a few possibilities. First-degree murder should be defined as the intentional killing of another person, save in self-defense, under duress, or as a result of the lawful actions of law enforcement officials. Second-degree murder is a killing that results from action that a prudent person would know involved a very high and an unreasonable risk of death. Voluntary manslaughter would be the verdict if the killing was the result of provocation, defined as behavior that would make a reasonable person immediately lose self-control. Involuntary manslaughter is a killing resulting from actions that a reasonable person knows creates a high risk of serious injury.[26]

These simple terms would delete from the homicide law of California and some other states words and phrases that have survived, undefined and with growing confusion, since the nineteenth century: "malice," "express malice, "implied malice," "premeditation," or having an "abandoned and malignant heart"; and new terms that have been recently invented by the courts, such as "intoxication," "battered women's syndrome," and "imperfect self-defense."

Apart from well-recognized justifications (such as self-defense or law enforcement) and excuses (such as necessity or insanity), all homicides would be clearly subject to simple tests: Was it intended? If intended, was the killer unreasonably provoked? If not intended, was the killing the result of actions that a reasonable person would know were risky?

Much of the difficulty of our homicide law arises from poorly drafted statutes, but much also depends on appeals courts modifying existing law in order to lessen—often for good reason—the burden of the existing law on a case the lawmakers had not foreseen. Courts know when they are thereby making new law; indeed, in the Conley case, the California Supreme Court stated in its opinion that it was doing just this.

I suggest that courts be required by statute to notify the legislature of the state of which they are a part of a new interpretation of statutory or common law, sending to the governor and the leaders of the upper and lower houses the ruling and the case in which it was formulated. By law the appropriate committees of each house would hold hearings on the ruling, inviting interested parties—prosecutors, defense attorneys, state executives, and interest groups—to present testimony on the circumstances in which the new ruling might be invoked so that a full and adversarial hearing might be held on the matter. The legislature would then either affirm, modify, or reject the ruling by statute.[27] In this way we can lessen the chances that a ruling that might properly have benefited Charles Flannel does not wrongly benefit Erik and Lyle Menendez.

Legislative review would not cure matters. Politicians can be as susceptible to the claims of new victims as are judges. After the first wave of court rulings upholding the battered woman syndrome, the California legislature passed a law in 1991 that declared expert testimony about it to be admissible whenever relevant because such testimony "shall not be considered a new scientific technique whose reliability is unproven."[28] For a legislature to decide when a scientific syndrome is "proven" is a bit bizarre, especially when, as George Fletcher has argued, they fail to specify the legal question to which the syndrome is the answer.[29] But at a minimum legislative review will broaden our understanding of new legal rules and increase the odds that a wider variety of opinion will be heard.

Criminal trials with high stakes and well-financed legal talent often generate an intense struggle between prosecution and defense over whether the jury will judge or explain.

With prosecutors looking for tough-minded jurors and defense attorneys for tender-minded ones, it often takes several days to choose a jury. In England, by contrast, jury selection usually consumes no more than a few minutes. The reason is that in England only the judge questions prospective jurors and then only to ascertain whether they have some obvious conflict of interest. "Do you know the defendant? Have you ever been charged with a similar crime?" To minimize the extent to which jurors are influenced by high-priced attempts to select them from the pool, the selection of American juries should be left entirely in the hands of the judge, with no peremptory challenges allowed to either the prosecution or defense.

Since 1990 California law has given the judge the right to conduct the voir dire but, alas, with a huge loophole: for "good cause" he or she can allow the opposing attorneys to "supplement the examination by such further inquiry as it deems proper" and to submit to prospective jurors "additional questions." The result was the notorious seventy-three-page questionnaire given to prospective jurors in the O. J. Simpson trial. Its purpose was not to weed out obviously incompetent or patently biased people but to enable lawyers to shape their strategy to appeal to the subjective state and personal inclinations of jurors. We should adopt the English position, and end attorney-guided voir dire and the attendant expense of consultants. In a criminal trial there is no reason why jury selection should take more than an hour.

England also provides guidance on running a trial. There the judge guides it by questioning witnesses, relegating motions to night sessions, and summarizing and commenting on the evidence before the jury begins its deliberations.

Federal rules already permit judges to do much of this, but appellate courts have discouraged judges from playing that role. Most states forbid judges from commenting on the evidence. Changing those laws and practices would not make trials less adversarial—the lawyers could still question witnesses and deliver summations—but it might make the presentation of the evidence more intelligible to the jury.

The appellate process ought to be more constrained, not to deny a defendant's right to an appeal, but to grant that right in a way that does not force all judges to worry that every evidentiary ruling they make will expose them to the possibility of reversal. The chief concern ought to be whether the appealed ruling does or does not raise an issue that materially affects the defendant's right to a fair trial. When Gladys Thomas was convicted only of reckless manslaughter when she killed her husband, it seems odd that an appeal should have been allowed on the grounds that she had not been allowed to present expert testimony from Dr. Lenore Walker. The implication seemed to be that such testimony might have justified an acquittal, an odd inference when someone kills another absent any threat to her life.

As regards expert witnesses, there is now no generally accepted way to screen prospective experts save by judicial ruling and trial cross-examination, and there seems to be no way to grant indigent defendants an opportunity to introduce experts at anything like the rate at which are summoned by wealthy suspects.

One possibility is to require that the judge select—and, where necessary, that the state pay for—experts. Federal evidentiary rules permit this, but the practice is not common.[30] It could be made more routine in various ways. A judge could select an independent expert, paid for by the state, to instruct the jury during the trial on the status of scientific testimony, especially that coming from novel approaches or the softer social sciences.[31] Some will claim that an independent expert will not really be objective but will nonetheless impress the jury with the claim of objectivity. This is an important objection, but it applies with even greater force to the present system of lawyer-selected experts, who are paid by, and largely beholden to, the side that chose them. Where court-appointed experts are used, they are typically involved in civil trials. In these controversies a lot of money is at risk. But in criminal trials human freedom and social protection are at risk, and so the case for having a court-appointed panel to advise the jury on the status of explanatory arguments is at least as strong.

A complementary measure would require that a side employing its own expert (where the claimed expertise is novel or extraordinary) be faced with an enhanced burden of proof. They might have to show, for example, that the proffered testimony is, by scientific standards, likely to be true beyond a reasonable doubt.[32] This is a high standard, but no higher than that imposed over time on fingerprint and DNA testing. It is just as important to impose it on claims about having been intoxicated or battered.

The boldest suggestion calls for the creation of independent bodies of experts who would be called upon before a trial to review novel scientific claims before they could be used in court. These might be ad hoc commissions summoned by a judge or periodic reviews of new scientific claims by a standing body such as the National Academy of Sciences.[33]

The most valuable approach to expert testimony, however, is for the trial judge to greet with skepticism any claim that social science can tell a jury much about *why* something happened. Very little such testimony tells the jury much that it does not know from common experience. But jurors can be bowled over by, or wrongly put off by, experts who claim that they know things beyond the jury's ken. Ordinary witnesses are found to be honest or dishonest, confident or heedless, dispassionate or reckless by the jurors' commonsense standards. Such witnesses are evaluated much as a person would evaluate a casual acquaintance. But expert witnesses are—well, experts. Some may be discounted, but it is not easily done. Jurors know little about science, and especially about the important scientific principle that a scholar never overstate or exaggerate a finding. When an expert witness speaks confidently of what "science" knows and admits of few, if any, exceptions to this "knowledge," the juror, as Kent Scheidegger has put it, is "at sea without a sextant." They are often at a loss to know how or whether to discount these claims, a fact clearly revealed in the first Menendez trial. Expert witnesses may be accepted by juries for the same reasons—manner, personality, appearance—that juries accept lay witnesses. But the best scientists may have a gruff manner, an unappealing personality, and an unattractive appearance; in science, personal attributes count for nothing in justifying a scientific claim. Jurors will not know that lay and expert witnesses must be judged by different standards.

And however the judge ensures that such an expert testifies only to general trends and not about the guilt or innocence of the defendant, the unstated message (and in some courts, the stated message) of their opinion will be understood to bear precisely on guilt or innocence even though they cannot—let me be clear, *they cannot*—know whether the defendant is in fact guilty or innocent.

LAWS, JURORS, AND JUDGMENT

Traditionally the law has drawn a careful line between what jurors need to know in order to judge and what they would like to know in order to explain. Of late that tendency has been relaxed in ways that permit jurors to do what they instinctively wish to do. It is only natural for people viewing a trial impartially to see it as a story enacted by people with complex personalities, difficult problems, and diverse backgrounds coping with emotion-laden circumstances.

The law has encouraged the explanatory rather than the judgmental mode of thought. But the law has not yet moved as far as some would like. Alive in several law schools are new ways of thinking that, if adopted by the courts, would move the law beyond urging juries to explain behavior to denying that juries (or at least certain juries) can either judge or explain. One of these ways is "critical race theory," developed by Derrick Bell, Regina Austin, Paul Butler, Richard Delgado, and others.[34] It argues that racism is so profoundly a part of American society that it determines how everyone sees the world. If white Americans see the world through their racist experiences, it cannot apply neutral laws in judging the behavior of nonwhites.

As an alternative to applying the law, many of these theorists urge that trials involve more "storytelling," by which they mean giving free rein to the expression of racially formed accounts of group experiences and group suffering. When Tawana Brawley, a young black woman in New York City, invented the story that she had been raped by white men, her cause was loudly championed by people who acted as if the truth or falsity of her story was irrelevant. And after it was shown to be false, her role in the story of black oppression was defended by some who wrote that even if she did fake the crime, her "condition" was the expression of "some" crime against her that entitled her to be the object of our grieving.[35] Paul Butler has carried this way of thinking to its logical conclusion. Writing in the *Yale Law Journal,* he urged African-American jurors to free guilty African-American defendants of nonviolent drug crimes.[36]

In a penetrating critique of this mode of thought, Jeffrey Rosen shows what should be obvious: Making the legal process the wholly subjective expression of group-determined minds ends the possibility of people from different groups agreeing about anything and converts the objectivity of the law into an expression of group beliefs. And that means the end of the rule of law.[37]

The lawyers who defended O. J. Simpson may not believe all of this, but they used their peremptory challenges to pick a jury in his criminal trial that consisted of eight African-American women—two-thirds of the jury in a city in which blacks are only one-ninth of the population. The defendant's jury advisers had said that black women believed Simpson was innocent. They were right. The "story" that was told was that the Los Angeles Police Department was so racist that it would not—*could* not—conduct an honest investigation of the murders. The story sold.

If human thought is wholly and narrowly the product of social construction, then there is no reason to limit storytelling to voices from below. Every voice will claim authority, including those from above. Such group thought once led white jurors to acquit whites who had killed blacks, whatever the evidence, and to convict blacks who may or may not have killed whites, whatever the evidence. And why stop with race? If race shapes our identity, so also does sex, age, wealth, and political ideology. This implies that men cannot judge women, adults cannot judge children, the rich cannot judge the poor, and liberals cannot judge conservatives.

African-Americans have suffered countless indignities. There are many ways by which some recompense can be offered. That supplied by the law, however, is of a special kind: a promise of fair treatment based on individual account-ability. For it to offer more, whether by excusing account-ability for some people defined by their group membership or by admitting group-based stories of their oppression, means the end of the law.

Appellate courts have not accepted any such broad claims. Probably they never will. But when they embrace an explanatory mode of thought, and do so in context of a lawyer-driven system of selecting jurors and "expert" wit-nesses, a context that implicitly favors wealthy or celebrated defendants, they come close to admitting through the back door what they excluded from the front.

For reasons of justice and deterrence, the law must draw a clear line, but that line ought to reflect the most widely shared moral sentiments of the people. The law claims to supply us with an objective standard, but a commitment to pure objectivity, giving people the same punishment though they act out of very different motives, risks stripping the law of its moral moorings in standards of justice. But the other extreme—entirely forsaking objective law in favor of shared group feelings—risks abandoning the neutral principles of the law, thereby unjustly punishing or absolving some peo-ple for thoughts, motives, and defects of character and weakening social control by telling some offenders that they can get away with it if they can come up with a good story.

The law is demanding and, to some people, extreme. Its prohibitions are addressed to people most lacking in self-control and least able to manage conflict. As many commentators have observed, the law does not display much empathy for the defendant.[38] But juries and judges often do, and so verdicts and penalties are adjusted to take into account human frailties and particular circumstances. That is at it should be, up to a point. The reason for making the law a series of relatively sharp, bright lines is to rein in our natural tendencies toward sympathy or vindictiveness.

Motivated by empathy for some group of disadvantaged defendants, some have pressed ardently for dulling those bright lines by defining new defenses or expanding old ones. But these advocates forget that a law that permits compassion also permits revenge. It took decades of insistence on the rule of law to induce some judges and juries to stop extending boundless understanding to whites who lynched blacks while denying any trace of sympathy to blacks who killed whites.

To avoid a well-intentioned repetition of this tragic mistake, it is important that we let neither science nor compassion decide legal precepts. We want to explain, the law seeks to judge; we want to see the world in shades of gray, the law defines it in black and white. We wish verdicts to encompass the full range of human circumstances, but the law can range only so widely before losing its power to focus our often diffuse sense of self-control. In extreme cases, where the law clearly does not fit, juries may nullify and judges may forgive, but only within the steady, lasting confines of a moral and legal order.

NOTES

Chapter 1: Faulty Experts

1. For example: "Crime in America," *The Economist,* 8 June 1996, 24, a report relying on the left-leaning Sentencing Project for data.

2. James Lynch, "Crime in International Perspective," in *Crime,* ed. James Q. Wilson and Joan Petersilia (San Francisco: Institute for Contemporary Studies, 1995), 32.

3. Ibid., 16, and David Farrington and Patrick Langan, "Changes in Crime and Punishment in England and Wales and America in the 1980s," *Justice Quarterly* 9 (1992): 6–46.

4. Lynch, "International Perspective," 34; Patrick A. Langan, "America's Soaring Prison Population," *Science* 251 (1991): 1568–73; Bureau of Justice Statistics, *Prison Sentences and Time Served for Violence* (April 1995): 1; California Department of Corrections, "Time Served on Prison Sentences, 1993," report dated May 1994, Sacramento, California.

5. John J. DiIulio Jr. and George A. Mitchell, "Who *Really* Goes to Prison in Wisconsin?" *Wisconsin Policy Research Institute Report* 9 (1996): 31–37.

6. James Fitzjames Stephens, *A History of the Criminal Law of England* (New York: Burt Franklin, 1973), 2:94 (first published in 1883).

7. See William Blackstone, *Commentaries on the Law of England,* 4:201; as cited in George Fletcher, *Rethinking Criminal Law* (Boston: Little, Brown & Co., 1978), 238.

8. Oliver Wendell Holmes, *The Common Law*, ed. Mark DeWolfe Howe (Cambridge, Mass.: Harvard University Press, 1963), 48 (first published in 1881).

9. Karl Popper, *The Logic of Scientific Discovery* (New York: Basic Books, 1959).

10. Federal Rules of Evidence, § 702.

11. *Frye v. United States*, 54 App. D.C. 47 (1923).

12. *People v. Stoll*, 49 Cal. 3rd 1136 (1989). The principal test used was the Minnesota Multiphasic Personality Inventory (MMPI). It is widely used and has substantial scientific value in assessing the personality of people. But neither it nor any other test can assess the guilt or innocence of a person. It is a scientific guide that produces an estimate of a person's personality but not a highly certain depiction of it.

13. Federal Rules of Evidence, § 702.

14. *Daubert v. Merrell Dow Pharmaceuticals*, 509 U.S. 579, 595 (1993). There is an extensive commentary on this case. See, for example, Bert Black, Francisco J. Ayala, and Carol Saffran-Banks, "Science and the Law in the Wake of *Daubert:* A New Search for Scientific Knowledge," *Texas Law Review* 72 (1994): 715–802; Clifford T. Hutchinson and Danny S. Ashby, *"Daubert v. Merrell Dow Pharmaceuticals, Inc.:* Redefining the Bases for Admissibility of Expert Testimony," *Cardozo Law Review* 15 (1994): 1875–1927.

15. Learned Hand, "Historical and Practical Considerations Regarding Expert Testimony," *Harvard Law Review* 15 (1901): 54.

16. Stanley Milgram, *Obedience to Authority* (New York: Harper & Row, 1974).

17. One important review of scientific testimony offers different proposals for managing complex (that is, hard to understand) and confusing (that is, controverted) testimony: "Confronting the New Challenges of Scientific Evidence," *Harvard Law Review* 108 (1995): 1481, 1583.

18. George P. Fletcher, *With Justice for Some* (Reading, Mass.: Addison-Wesley, 1995), 47.

19. The same point is made in Donald L. Horowitz, *The Courts and Social Policy* (Washington, D.C.: Brookings Institution, 1977), 275.

20. Fletcher, "With Justice," 234.

21. "Confronting the New Challenges," 1493.

22. *Wells v. Ortho Pharmaceutical Corp.,* 788 F.2d, 741, 745 (1985); Black, Ayala, and Saffran-Brinks, "*Daubert:* A New Search," 719.

23. Cited in Paul C. Giannelli, "'Junk Science': The Criminal Cases," *Journal of Criminal Law and Criminology* 84 (1993): 113–14.

24. *Barefoot v. Estelle,* 463 U.S. 880, 901 (1983).

25. Giannelli, "'Junk Science,'" 118–19.

26. *Ake v. Oklahoma,* 470 U.S. 68 (1985).

27. Giannelli, "'Junk Science,'" 120–25.

28. Federal Rule of Criminal Procedure 15.

29. *National Law Journal,* 11 June 1990, 30.

30. David Faigman, "To Have and Have Not: Assessing the Value of Social Science to the Law as Science and Policy," *Emory Law Journal* 38 (1989): 1013.

Chapter 2: Self-Control

1. Quoted in Mike Weiss, *Double Play: The San Francisco City Hall Killings* (Reading, Mass.: Addison-Wesley, 1984), 351. See also reported testimony, 364.

2. By ballot initiative California voters abolished the diminished capacity defense in 1982, almost certainly in reaction against the White verdict.

3. Alan M. Dershowitz, *The Abuse Excuse* (Boston: Little, Brown & Co., 1994), 321–41.

4. Richard Delgado, "'Rotten Social Background:' Should the Criminal Law Recognize a Defense of Severe Environmental Deprivation?" *Law and Inequality Journal* 3 (1985): 9; David L. Bazelon, "The Morality of the Criminal Law," *Southern California Law Review* 49 (1976): 385.

5. *People v. Wells,* 202 P.2d 53 (1949); *People v. Conley,* 411 P.2d 911 (1966).

6. *People v. Conley,* 411 P.2d 911, at 918 (1966).

7. Ibid., 916.

8. *People v. Wolff,* 394 P.2d 959, 976 (1964).

9. Peter Arenella, "The Diminished Capacity and Diminished Responsibility Defenses: Two Children of a Doomed Marriage," *Columbia Law Review* 77 (1977): 835, 844.

10. Ibid., 848.

11. The Riot Act, a law passed in England in 1715, made it a felony for twelve or more people to assemble unlawfully and disturb the peace. Merely assembling exposed one to felony charges even if the unlawful act committed by the assembly was a misdemeanor.

12. Paul H. Robinson, "Riot Responsibility," *New York State Bar Journal* (January 1994): 6–8; "Note: Feasibility and Admissibility of Mob Mentality Defenses," *Harvard Law Review* 108 (1995): 1111–26.

13. Douglas Murdoch, R. O. Pihl, and Deborah Ross, "Alcohol and Crimes of Violence," *International Journal of the Addictions* 25 (1990): 1065–81.

14. California Penal Code, § 22(a). See also Model Penal Code, § 2.08.

15. See, for example, *People v. Potter,* 77 Cal. App. 3rd 45, at 51 (1978).

16. *People v. Guillet,* 69 N.W. 2d 140 (1955).

17. California Penal Code, § 22(b).

18. Wayne R. LaFave and Austin W. Scott, Jr., *Criminal Law,* 2 ed. (St. Paul, Minn.: West Publishing, 1986), § 4.10.

19. Ibid., 389; *Heidemann v. U.S., 259* F.2d 943 (1958) on robbery; *People v. Guillet,* 342 Mich. 1 (1955) on rape.

20. LaFave and Scott, *Criminal Law,* 390, and the cases cited thereon at note 25.

21. My reading suggests that in about five states, voluntary intoxication will excuse any required element of an offense and in another seventeen it can excuse specific but not general intent. I know of only five states where it cannot be used as the basis of any excuse. See Paul H. Robinson, *Criminal Law Defenses,* vol. 2 (St. Paul, Minn.: West, 1984), § 65 and appended supplement through 1995.

22. Justice Fortas dissenting for four justices in *Powell v. Texas,* 392 U.S. 514 (1968) at 567–68. A similar view is expressed by Judge Wright in his dissent, for four judges, in *U.S. v. Moore,* 486 F.2d 1139, at 1257 (D.C. Circ., 1973).

23. Cf. Herbert Fingarette, *Heavy Drinking* (Berkeley and Los Angeles: University of California Press, 1988).

24. *State v. Egelhoff,* 900 P.2d 260 (1995).

25. The states are Arizona, Arkansas, Delaware, Georgia, Hawaii, Mississippi, Missouri, Montana, South Carolina, and Texas.

26. *Montana v. Egelhoff,* 64 U.S. Law Week 4500 (1996).

27. Joyce Hopkins, Marsha Marcus, and Susan B. Campbell, "Postpartum Depression: A Critical Review," *Psychological Bulletin* 95 (1984): 498–515. For a discussion of cases involving PPD, see Laura E. Reece, "Mothers Who Kill: Postpartum Disorders and Criminal Infanticide," *UCLA Law Review* 38 (1991): 699–757.

28. American Psychiatric Association, *DSM-IV* (1994), § 309.81. See also Michael J. Davidson, "Post-Traumatic Stress Disorder," *William and Mary Law Review* 29 (1988): 415–40; C. Peter Erlinder, "Paying the Price for Vietnam: Post-Traumatic Stress Disorder and Criminal Behavior," *Boston College Law Review* 25 (1984): 305–47; James Carroll, "Post-Traumatic Stress Disorder as an Insanity Defense in Vermont," *Vermont Law Review* 9 (1984): 69–100.

29. See the cases summarized in Davidson, "Post-Traumatic Stress," 422–23, and Erlinder, "Paying the Price," pp. 317–31.

30. *State v. Cocuzza,* No. 1484–79 (Middlesex County, New Jersey, 1981).

31. Reece, "Mothers Who Kill," 742, discussing *State v. Householder,* No. 86-F–6 (Jefferson County Circuit Court, West Virginia, 1986).

32. *Regina v. English,* (Norwich Crown Court, Nov. 10, 1981), as described in Christina L. Hosp, "Has the PMS Defense Gained a Legitimate Toehold in Virginia Criminal Law?" *George Mason Law Review* 14 (1991): 429–30.

33. *Regina v. Craddock,* 1 C.L. 49 (1980); *Regina v Smith,* No. 1/A/82 (C.A. Crim Div., April 27, 1982), both as reported in Lee Solomon, "Premenstrual Syndrome," *Maryland Law Review* 54 (1995): 582–83. (Between 1980 and 1982 Craddock changed her name to Smith.)

34. Solomon, "Premenstrual Syndrome," 583.

35. M'Naghten's Case, 8 English Reports 718 (1843) as quoted in LaFave and Scott, *Criminal Law,* 311.

36. Cf. Abraham Goldstein, *The Insanity Defense* (New Haven: Yale University Press, 1967), 59–62; Robert Waleder, "Psychiatry and the Problem of Criminal Responsibility," *University of Pennsylvania Law Review,* 101 (1952): 384.

37. *Durham v. U.S.,* 214 F.2d 862 (D.C. Cir. 1954). The Durham rule was adumbrated by a New Hampshire state court ruling in the nineteenth century: *State v. Jones,* 50 N.H. 369 (1871).

38. American Law Institute, *Model Penal Code,* section 4.01. The Code's provisions were widely adopted by many states and, for a while, most federal appeals courts. But Congress later decided that federal courts should use its variant of the M'Naghten Rule.

39. Joseph Livermore and Paul Meehl, "The Virtues of M'Naghten," *Minnesota Law Review* 51 (1967): 789–856.

40. Michael S. Moore, *Law and Psychiatry* (Cambridge: Cambridge University Press, 1984); Moore, "Causation and the Excuses," *California Law Review* 73 (1985): 1091–1149; Moore, *Act and Crime: The Philosophy of Action and Its Implications for Criminal Law* (Oxford: Clarendon Press, 1993).

41. The debate over the status of moral agency in the law is a lively one. Compare Peter Arenella, "Character, Choice, and Moral Agency," *Social Philosophy and Policy* 7 (1990): 59–83, with Michael S. Moore, "Choice, Character, and Excuse," *Social Philosophy and Policy* 7 (1990): 29–58.

42. Oliver Wendell Holmes, *The Common Law,* ed. Mark DeWolfe Howe (Cambridge, Mass.: Harvard University Press, 1963), 43.

43. Cf. H. L. A. Hart, *Punishment and Responsibility* (Oxford: Clarendon Press, 1968), chap. 2; Livermore and Meehl, "The Virtues"; Moore, "Causation and its Excuses."

44. Moore, "Causation and Its Excuses," 1129: "The difference between compulsion and causation comes to this: compulsion interferes with practical reasoning."

45. For evidence on these factors, see James Q. Wilson and Richard J. Herrnstein, *Crime and Human Nature* (New York: Simon & Schuster, 1985); Adrian Raine, *The Psychopathology of Crime* (San Diego: Academic Press, 1993); and Deborah W. Denno, "Gender, Crime, and

Criminal Law Defenses," *Journal of Criminal Law and Criminology* 85 (1994): 80–180.

Chapter 3: Self-Defense

1. Lois Timnick and Paul Feldman, "Son Acquitted of Trying to Murder Abusive Father," *Los Angeles Times*, 11 October 1986, 1.

2. California Penal Code, title 8, chap. 1, § 197, 198; *Garcia v. State*, 667 P.2d 1148 (Wyoming, 1983).

3. *Ibn-Tamas v. United States*, 407 A.2d 626 (1979); *Ibn-Tamas v. United States*, 455 A.2d 893 (1983).

4. See *Dyas v. United States*, 376 A.2d 827.

5. *Ibn-Tamas v. United States*, 407 A.2d 626, at 634.

6. *U.S. v. Hearst*, 412 F. Supp. 889, at 890 (1976).

7. The federal judges were not alone in believing, without evidence, that jurors cannot grasp the predicament of a battered woman. Early state judicial decisions also made this assertion, citing the nonevidence in Dr. Walker's book. See *Bechtel v. State*, 840 P.2d 1 (Oklahoma, 1982) and *State v. Hodges*, 716 P.2d 563 (Kansas, 1986).

8. *State v. Kelly*, 478 A.2d 364, at 370 (1984).

9. Lenore E. Walker, *The Battered Woman* (New York: Harper & Row, 1979). The court directs the reader to pages 19 to 31. These pages contain no data or studies confirming the existence of the myth. See also James R. Acker and Hans Toch, "Battered Women, Straw Men, and Expert Testimony: A Comment on *State v. Kelly*," *Criminal Law Bulletin* 22 (1985): 125–55.

10. See Edith Green, Alan Raits, and Heidi Linblad, "Jurors' Knowledge of Battered Women," *Journal of Family Violence* 4 (1989): 115.

11. Martin Seligman, et al., "Alleviation of Learned Helplessness in the Dog," *Journal of Abnormal Psychology* 73 (1968): 256–62.

12. Martin Seligman, *Helplessness* (San Francisco: Freeman, 1975); Seligman, et al., "Learned Helplessness in Humans: Critique and Reformulation," *Journal of Abnormal Psychology* 87 (1978): 49–74.

13. Lenore E. Walker, *Terrifying Love: Why Battered Women Kill and How Society Responds* (New York: HarperCollins, 1989), 49–53.

14. Mary Ann Dutton, "Understanding Women's Responses to Domestic Violence: A Redefinition of Battered Women's Syndrome," *Hofstra Law Review* 21 (1993): 1191–1241, at 1225–31.

15. B. J. Rounsaville, "Theories in Marital Violence: Evidence From a Study of Battered Women," *Victimology* 3 (1978): 11–31; Richard J. Gelles, "Abused Wives: Why Do They Stay?" *Journal of Marriage and the Family* 38 (1976): 659–68. See also Don Dutton and Susan Lee Painter, "Traumatic Bonding: The Development of Emotional Attachments in Battered Women and Other Relationships of Intermittent Abuse," *Victimology* 6 (1981): 139–55.

16. Michael J. Strube, "The Decision to Leave an Abusive Relationship: Empirical Evidence and Theoretical Issues," *Psychological Bulletin* 104 (1988): 236–50, at 243.

17. Lenore E. Walker, *The Battered Woman Syndrome* (New York: Springer, 1984), 78–80. See also Robert F. Schopp, Barbara J. Sturgis, and Megan Sullivan, "Battered Women Syndrome, Expert Testimony, and the Distinction Between Justification and Excuse," *University of Illinois Law Review* 1994 (1994): 45–113, at 55–59.

18. Summarized in Schopp, et al., "Justification and Excuse," 60–64.

19. Comment, "Battered Women Who Kill Their Abusers," *Harvard Law Review* 106 (1993): 1585–86.

20. California Evidence Code, § 1107(B); Ohio Revised Code Annotated, § 2901.06(A)1–2.

21. *People v. Humphrey*, 1996 Cal. Lexis 4222 (1996).

22. Walker, *The Battered Woman Syndrome* 215–21; see also Schopp, et al., "Justification and Excuse," 55.

23. Walker, *The Battered Woman Syndrome,* 78–81. This criticism is developed by Anne E. Coughlin, "Excusing Women," *California Law Review,* 82 (1994): 85–86.

24. Walker, *Terrifying Love,* 102.

25. This point is developed in Schopp, et al., "Justification and Excuse," 71–73.

26. Cf. *State v. Hundley,* 693 P.2d 475 (Kansas, 1985); *State v. Kelly,* 478 A.2d 364, at 372 (New Jersey, 1984).

27. Anne M. Coughlin, "Excusing Women," *California Law Review* 82 (1994): 50–51.

28. Ibid., 58–59.

29. Susan Estrich, "Defending Women," *Michigan Law Review* 88 (1990): 1431. She is here criticizing Cynthia Gillespie, *Justifiable Homicide: Battered Women, Self-Defense, and the Law* (Columbus: Ohio State University Press, 1989).

30. *People v. Flannel,* 25 Cal. 3rd 668 (1979); *In re Christian S.,* 7 Cal. 4th 872 (1994); Kevin Patrick McGee, "The Absence of Malice? *In re Christian S.,* the Second Wind of the Imperfect Self-Defense Doctrine," *Golden Gate University Law Review* 25 (1995): 297–330.

31. *People v. Flannel,* 603 P. 2d 1 (1979), CH4.

32. Jury instructions as quoted in Holly Maguigan, "Battered Women and Self-Defense," *University of Pennsylvania Law Review* 140 (1991): 410 n108.

33. See George P. Fletcher, *A Crime of Self-Defense: Bernard Goetz and the Law on Trial* (New York: Free Press, 1988).

34. *State v. Leidholm,* 334 N.W. 2d 811, 817–819 (1983). The courts in other several other states have embraced the subjective test of imminence. See *State v. Gallegos,* 719 P. 2d 1268, at 1271 (New Mexico, 1986) and *State v. Hodges,* 716 P. 2d 563, at 571 (Kansas, 1986).

35. For example, *State v. Wanrow,* 559 P2d 548 (1977).

36. *State v. Norman,* 378 S.E.2d 8 (1989).

37. Richard A. Rosen, "On Self-Defense, Imminence, and Women Who Kill Their Batterers," *North Carolina Law Review* 71 (1993): 371–411; Paul H. Robinson, *Criminal Law Defenses,* vol. 2 (St. Paul, Minn.: West, 1984), 78.

38. *State v. Leaphart,* 673 S.W. 2d 870 (1983).

39. Walker, *Terrifying Love,* 286–93.

40. *State v. Martin,* 666 S.W. 2d 895 (1984).

41. *Commonwealth v. Kacsmar,* 617 A. 2d 725 (1992).

42. Hazel Thornton, *Hung Jury: The Diary of a Menendez Juror* (Philadelphia: Temple University Press, 1995), 24–55.

43. Alan W. Schefil, "Legal Commentary on the Diary" in Thornton, *Hung Jury,* 136–38.

Chapter 4: Changing Conceptions of Responsibility

1. Thomas Andrew Green, *Verdict According to Conscience* (Chicago: University of Chicago Press, 1985), 32. See also Douglas Hay, "Crime and Justice in Eighteenth- and Nineteenth-Century England," in *Crime and Justice,* vol. 2, eds. Norval Morris and Michael Tonry, (Chicago: University of Chicago Press, 1980), 45–84.

2. Hay, "Crime and Justice," 50, n4.

3. J. M. Beattie, *Crime and the Courts in England, 1660–1800* (Oxford: Clarendon Press, 1986), 619.

4. Ibid., 630.

5. Ibid., 632.

6. Martin J. Wiener, *Reconstructing the Criminal: Culture, Law, and Policy in England, 1830–1914* (Cambridge: Cambridge University Press, 1990).

7. Ibid., 50.

8. Ibid., 48.

9. Ibid.

10. Hay, "Crime and Justice," 57.

11. Wiener, *Reconstructing,* 38–45.

12. F. M. L. Thompson, *The Rise of Respectable Society* (London: Fontana, 1988), 260; Wiener, *Reconstructing,* 179.

13. Wiener, *Reconstructing,* chap. 9, esp. 357–61.

14. Homicide Act of 1957, 5&6 Eliz. 2 c ll, § 2, 3.

15. *Criminal Statistics, England and Wales, 1994* (London: Home Office), 1995, Table 4.2.

16. Ibid., Table 2.16; *Prison Statistics, England and Wales, 1993* (London: Home Office, 1995), Table 4.7.

17. Christopher Nuttall and Ken Pease, "Changes in the Use of Imprisonment in England and Wales, 1950–1991," *Criminal Law Review* (1994): 318.

18. Ibid., 321–22.

19. David P. Farrington and Patrick A. Langan, "Changes in Crime and Punishment in England and America in the 1980s," *Justice Quarterly* 9 (1992): 14.

20. Lawrence M. Friedman, *Crime and Punishment in American*

History (New York: Basic Books, 1993), 73–76, 127–32. See also Charles E. Rosenberg, "Sexuality, Class and Role in Nineteenth-Century America," *American Quarterly* 25 (1973): 131.

21. *Statistical Abstract of the United States, 1972* (Washington, D.C.: Government Printing Office, 1972), 161.

22. *Statistical Abstract of the United States, 1995* (Washington, D.C.: Government Printing Office, 1995), 217.

23. Patrick A. Langan, "America's Soaring Prison Population," *Science* 251 (1991): 1568–73.

24. James Q. Wilson, "Crime and Punishment in England," *Public Interest* 43 (1976): 3–25.

25. Criminal Justice Act 1991, § 1.

26. *Regina v. Cox,* 2 All ER 19 (1992).

27. Joshua Rozenberg, *The Search for Justice* (London: Hodder and Stoughton, 1994), 133.

28. See Morton Keller, *Regulating a New Society: Public Policy and Social Change in America, 1900–1933* (Cambridge, Mass.: Harvard University Press, 1994), 160–61, and *University of Pennsylvania Law Review* 59 (1911): 251–52.

29. From data gathered by Loretta Damron of the London office of the Pepperdine Law School. See also Rozenberg, *The Search*, 132.

30. Rozenberg, *The Search*, 7.

31. *Beckford v. Queen,* (P.C.) Ap. Cas. 130 (1988), 143–44.

Chapter 5: Law and Responsibility

1. Harry Kalven and Hans Zeisel, *The American Jury* (Chicago: University of Chicago Press, 1966).

2. Norman J. Finkel, *Commonsense Justice: Jurors' Notions of the Law* (Cambridge, Mass.: Harvard University Press, 1995), 146–50.

3. M. J. Brondino, et al., "Defendant Variables Affecting Juror Verdicts in Cases Where Battered Women Kill Their Husbands," unpublished paper cited in Finkel, *Commonsense Justice,* 253.

4. California Evidence Code, § 352.

5. Michael H. Graham, *Tightening the Reins of Justice in America*

(Westport, Conn.: Greenwood Press, 1983), 3; Gordon Van Kessel, "Adversary Excesses in the American Criminal Trial," *Notre Dame Law Review* 67 (1992): 469–73.

6. Edward H. Levi, *An Introduction to Legal Reasoning* (Chicago: University of Chicago Press, 1949), 1–3.

7. *Berkey v. Third Avenue Railway Co.,* 155 N.E. 58, 61 (1926), as cited in Levi, *Legal Reasoning,* 8 n10.

8. 18 United States Code 398.

9. *Athanasaw v. United States,* 227 US 326 (1913); *Caminetti v. United States,* 242 US 470 (1917); *Cleveland v. United States,* 329 US 14 (1946).

10. *People v. Flannel,* 603 P.2d 1 (1979).

11. For example: *People v. Ceja,* 26 Cal. App. 4th 78 (1994); *People v. Minifie,* 38 Cal. App. 4th 597 (1995); *People v. DeLeon,* 10 Cal. App. 4th 815 (1992); *People v. Cameron,* 30 Cal. App. 4th 591 (1994); *People v. Curtis,* 30 Cal. App. 4th 1337 (1994); *People v. Sekona,* 27 Cal. App. 4th 443 (1994).

12. *In re Christian,* 7 Cal. 4th 768 (1994). The Court also quoted in support of its view *People v. Aris,* 215 Cal. App. 3d (1989).

13. *People v. Aris,* 215 Cal. App. 3rd 1178, 1187 (1989).

14. Dissent of Chief Justice Lucas in *In re Christian,* 7 Cal. 4th 768, 786–96 (1994).

15. R. U. Singh, "History of the Defence of Drunkenness in English Criminal Law," *Law Quarterly Review* 49 (1933): 528–46.

16. Francis Bowers Sayre, "Mens Rea," *Harvard Law Review* 45 (1932): 1013–15.

17. Steven S. Nemerson, "Alcoholism, Intoxication, and the Criminal Law," *Cardozo Law Review* 10 (1988): 414.

18. Chester N. Mitchell, "The Intoxicated Offender—Refuting the Legal and Medical Myths," *International Journal of Law and Psychiatry* 11 (1988): 77–103.

19. Jerome Hall, "Intoxication and Criminal Responsibility," *Harvard Law Review* 57 (1944): 1045–84.

20. Hall, "Intoxication," 1054. Cf. Monrad G. Paulsen, "Intoxication as a Defense To Crime," *University of Illinois Law Forum* (Spring 1961): 1–24.

21. *Clarkson v. The Queen*, 25 C.C.C. (3d) 207 (1986).

22. *Regina v. Canute*, 80 C.C.C. (3rd) 403 (1993).

23. This point is conceded by Steven S. Nemerson, "Alcoholism," 440–43, 461–63.

24. *State v. Wanrow*, 559 P.2d 548 (Washington, 1977); *State v. Leidholm*, 334 N.W.2d 811 (North Dakota, 1983); *State v. Hodges*, 716 P.2d 263 (Kansas, 1986).

25. *People v. Wolff*, 394 P.2d 959, 976 (1964).

26. I am indebted for these suggestions to Charles L. Hobson of the Criminal Justice Legal Foundation. See his "Reforming California's Homicide Law," *Pepperdine Law Review* 23 (1996): 495–563. I leave out of my brief account the complexities attached to the felony murder rule and modify his idea by attaching the notion of legislative review.

27. Robert A. Katzmann reports on an experiment in which courts transmitted opinions interpreting statutes to the relevant congressional committees in "Bridging the Statutory Gulf Between Courts and Congress," *Georgetown Law Journal* 80 (1992): 653–69, and Katzmann, *Courts and Congress* (Washington, D.C.: Brookings Institution, 1997).

28. George P. Fletcher, *With Justice for Some* (Reading, Mass.: Addison-Wesley, 1995), 135, quoting California Evidence Code, § 1107(a), 1107(b).

29. Ibid.

30. Federal Rules of Evidence 706.

31. Steven M. Egedal, "The *Frye* Doctrine and Relevancy Approach Controversy: An Empirical Examination," *Georgetown Law Journal* 74 (1986): 1787; "Confronting the Challenges of Scientific Evidence," *Harvard Law Review* 108 (1995): 1589; Samuel R. Gross, "Expert Evidence," *Wisconsin Law Review* 1991 (1991): 1220–32.

32. Paul C. Giannelli, "The Admissibility of Novel Scientific Evidence: *Frye v. United States*, a Half-Century Later," *Columbia Law Review* 80 (1980): 1247–49.

33. Ibid., 1231–32.

34. A leading example is Derrick Bell, *Race, Racism, and American Law*, 3d ed. (Boston: Little, Brown, 1992).

35. Patricia Williams, as quoted in Jeffrey Rosen, "The Bloods and the Crits," *The New Republic* (December 9, 1996): 32.

36. Paul Butler, "Racially Based Jury Nullification: Black Power in Criminal Justice System," *Yale Law Journal* 105 (1995): 677–725. See also Eleanor Brown, "The Tower of Babel: Bridging the Divide Between Critical Race Theory and 'Mainstream' Civil Rights Scholarship," *Yale Law Journal* 105 (1995): 513–47.

37. Rosen, "Bloods and Crits," 32.

38. Stephen J. Schulhofer, "The Gender Question in Criminal Law," *Social Philosophy and Policy* 7 (1990): 112–13.

INDEX

Religious involvement, crime caused by lack of, 43

Responsibility. *See* Diminished responsibility; Personal responsibility; Social responsibility

Retribution, in Anglo-American law, 84–85

Riot Act, 27, 116*n*11

Robbery, in English law, 77

Rosen, Jeffrey, 110

"Rotten social background" defense, 23

Rule 702, 11

Scheidegger, Kent, 108

Science: intoxication and, 99–100; law and, 8–9, 75, 76, 99–100; social science versus, 13–16; surviving falsification and, 13–16. *See also* Expert testimony

Scott, Austin, 31

Self-control, 22–43, 43, 112; American law and, 78–79; diminished responsibility and, 23, 24–28, 77, 85–87, 102; English law and, 70–78; excusing failures of, 43; insanity and, 2, 3, 7, 36–43, 118*n*38; as murder justification, 7; White trail and, 3, 5, 22–24, 26, 42, 97, 102. *See also* Depression; Intoxication; Stress

Self-defense, 44–69; battered child syndrome and, 47; battered person syndrome and, 66–67; expert testimony and, 68–69; imperfect, 59–62, 91–97, 103; Richard John Jahnke and, 46–47, 48; Sociz Junatanov and, 47, 48; law of, 48–56; Erik

and Lyle Menendez and, 44–46, 47–48, 60, 68–69; as murder justification, 7; necessity and, 64–66; nonconfrontational killings and, 62–66; perfect, 59; psychosexual abuse and, 2, 45, 91. *See also* Battered women's syndrome

Seligman, Martin, 52, 53

Simpson, O. J., 5, 12, 105, 110

Single-parent family, crime caused by living in, 43

Social responsibility, 1–2, 84–88. *See also* Excuses

Social science: banning testimony from experts in, 20–21; criminal law versus, 7–8; science versus, 13–16. *See also* Expert testimony

Soft science. *See* Social science

Specific intent crime, 28, 98–99, 100; intoxication and, 29, 30–31

Statutory law, court notifying legislature of new interpretation of, 104

Steroid defense, 23, 24, 35, 36

Stillings, Wayne, 65

Story telling, 109–11, 112

Stress, posttraumatic stress disorder and, 2, 23, 33–34, 43, 85

Subjectivity, self-defense and, 63

Substantial capacity test, Model Penal Code and, 37–38, 118*n*38

Supreme Court: on expert testimony, 11–12, 16, 19, 20, 114*n*14; on indigent defendants, 20; on intoxication, 31–32, 32; on science surviving falsification, 16

Syndrome science, 20–21; battered child syndrome, 47; battered person syndrome, 66–67; fetal